The Rose Hedge

The Rose Hedge

ELIZABETH ELGIN

ROBERT HALE • LONDON

ISBN 0 7090 5911 6

Robert Hale Limited
Clerkenwell House
Clerkenwell Green
London EC1R 0HT

Typeset by Pitfold Design, Hindhead, Surrey.
Printed in Great Britain by St Edmundsbury Press, Bury St
Edmunds, Suffolk. Bound by WBC Book Manufacturers Limited,
Bridgend, Mid-Glamorgan.

One

It was entirely the fault of the newspaper advertisement. *Southgate Lodge, Abbeyfield.* The printed words leaped out at Liri and in that instant Gideon's mouth was hard on hers again and the air was filled with the scent of new-cut hay.

Secluded, urged the advertisement, *but not isolated. A rare opportunity to secure a small, delightful property in beautiful countryside.*

Liri had no need to read on. To her, Abbeyfield had never ceased to be beautiful. Even now there was hardly a day on which it did not reach out to remind her. The village green where geese grazed; the rose-brick cottages as old as the Spanish Armada and Queen's Reach, of course, standing behind the high yew hedges her grandfather once clipped each year at Martinmas. Queen's Reach; a house Liri once loved as if it had been her own.

'Take a look at this, Con. It's where I was born – well,

in the gardener's cottage on the estate.' She passed over the paper. 'I'm going up there, to see it.'

'But it's for sale!' Connie Davies's face registered dismay. 'What on earth do you want with a lodge in North Yorkshire?'

'I *don't* want it. I just want to look. And I won't come to any harm,' Liri teased. 'There aren't many highwaymen about now and I speak the language fluently. The natives'll be friendly, so don't worry.'

'OK. Point taken. But promise you won't get any peculiar ideas? I get uneasy when you get that look in your eyes.'

'I was only thinking it might be nice to see Queen's Reach again,' Liri shrugged. 'I won't do anything silly. London's where I live, now. It'll be a – a sentimental journey, that's all.'

'And nothing at all to do with James?' Connie's eyes narrowed with suspicion, remembering that last night there had been words, and James had left with a slamming of doors and a screaming of tyres.

'Not that it's any business of mine, but I'd mention it in passing if I were you. Unless you're going up there to kick over the traces, Roz?'

Roz. She was Rosamund Haslington now, Liri reminded herself and she *didn't* want to buy a tiny gate-lodge in delightful countryside; only to see Queen's Reach one last time, then forget, because she was eight years older now and eight years wiser and when she saw Queen's Reach again she must be in command of her emotions; so completely in command, she stressed, that if she should meet Gideon Whitaker —

But Gideon would not be there. He couldn't be, because after 400 years the Whitakers were selling out, it seemed; giving up the land on which their long-ago ancestor built his small, squat farmhouse and named it for the queen who bestowed it. And every generation since had added to it until they became rich and powerful and owned all Abbeyfield.

Yet now it would appear that parts of Queen's Reach were being sold and it was quite delightful to think that she, the gardener's granddaughter, was arranging to view the gate-lodge on the southern tip of the estate.

Not that she intended buying – it would be ridiculous even to consider it – but here was a heaven-sent opportunity to see the rose hedge her grandfather had planted and the drift of lilies-of-the-valley he scattered beneath it; the small, white flowers from which her name had evolved. She must see it just once more, she yearned, before she said yes to James.

Immediately her mind pulled down a curtain. Best she should think about the lilies. It was too early yet for them to be flowering, but perhaps she would see their pale green tips breaking through the soil.

Liriconfancies Grandpa had called them. 'Pale and tender-looking like you, child, but tough as old boots. One of those little lilies can push its way through a crack in a flagstone.'

So it seemed natural she should become Liri. Even now it suited her better than her real name because she had remained pale and fair and slight, and even if she had not been quite as tough as those old boots, at least she had been able to keep up with Gideon; a considerable achievement, considering he'd been seven years older. Gideon would be 32 now, she brooded. He'd have been married to Fenella for almost —

'Hey. ' Snapping fingers burst the bubble of Liri's daydream. 'Where were you?'

'Miles away, Con. *Years* away . . . .'

'Hmm. It figures.' She lifted an enquiring eyebrow. 'You're still a bit of a mystery, Roz. Not that I'm prying,' she added hastily.

'I know, Con, and I *will* tell you – one day . . . .'

When she had been to Abbeyfield, that was. When she had seen Queen's Reach again, and the rose hedge. When she finally knew she could think of Gideon and speak of Gideon and not weep inside her.

The York estate agent offered to drive Liri to Abbeyfield.

'No trouble, Miss Haslington. I've other business in that direction as it happens.'

He had given her a brochure but she left it unopened on her lap, looking around her at the narrow old streets, loving her city as she had always loved it, feeling so at home she might never have been away.

Yet it was almost eight years since she left. She had gone quietly, furtively almost, telling no-one where she was going.

'It's a beautiful little village,' the agent ventured. 'It isn't every day a property in Abbeyfield comes on the market.'

'I wonder why they're selling Southgate?' Liri side-stepped the sales talk. 'They've been at Queen's Reach since Tudor times and it isn't like them at all.'

'The Whitakers, you mean? Oh, they've left.' He dismissed them as if 400 years counted for nothing. 'What's left of the estate is being restored by a builder, now.' He looked pointedly down at the unread brochure. 'There's land with the lodge, by the way. Only four acres, but handy if you ride.'

'I don't.' Never again since Gideon's pony had thrown her.

'No matter. It shouldn't be a problem. The farmers around Abbeyfield are greedy for extra acreage. Sell off those fields and the lodge'll come a whole lot cheaper.' A yearning expression crossed his face. 'Pity it couldn't be sold for development. The money those four acres would be worth as building land doesn't bear thinking about.

You'd be comfortable for the rest of your days.'

Liri smiled, wondering what he would say if he knew that already she was doing very nicely, thanks all the same. Now she was award-winning Rosamund Haslington and rapidly establishing herself as a textile designer.

'I was born in Abbeyfield,' it pleased her to tell him. 'And on the Queen's Reach estate, too. My grandfather was head gardener there.'

She was enjoying herself, now. She had even stopped feeling guilty for bringing the man on a wasted journey, because if there had been *forty* acres of land with Southgate Lodge she would not be offering for it. But Connie had come dangerously near the truth. True, there were no traces to kick over, but there *was* a ghost to be laid; the ghost of a past, perfidious love. But it had all happened so long ago, Liri sighed, so it shouldn't be too difficult. Oh, please, not *too* difficult?

Liri asked the estate agent to drive slowly through the village willing herself to be calm. On the surface little had changed except that now a motor-mower appeared to have replaced the nibbling geese on the green and the oak trees at the far end of the village seemed to have grown taller. She glanced fondly at the church as they drove past and at the clock, still five minutes slow. And then she saw the high yew hedges ahead and her heart began to pound.

She was back. Passionately she had vowed never to return, yet she was home again, and near to tears.

'Not much farther, Miss Haslington.'

'I know.' Her voice was low-pitched with emotion. 'I used to live here, remember?'

'Then you'll be familiar with Southgate Lodge?'

'Yes. Nanny Brightwell retired there after – after

Matthew and Gideon Whitaker grew up. I lived in Pond Cottage, though – next door to the gamekeeper's house.'

'You're in for a surprise, then.' He stopped the car at the top of Meadowsweet Lane. 'Now can I leave you alone for about half an hour? There's a farmer I want to see. You'll be all right?'

'No problem.' She held out her hand for the key. Half an hour would be fine; long enough for her to see Queen's Reach and take one last look at the rose hedge; see it for the very last time. 'About three o'clock, shall we say?'

Southgate Lodge was empty and hollow and it was hard to imagine that here she had once spent so many happy times; innocently happy times when she and Gideon had been brother and sister, almost; before that first naive kiss had brought a new awareness and a wonderful, exciting strangeness.

She had come often with Gideon to visit Nanny, and they toasted teacakes on a long brass fork and laughed a lot. And she remembered the firelight and the warm, glowing coals and was glad the old stone fireplace was still there, and the mullioned windows, too, at either end of the room.

And now, if she wished hard enough, would she hear the echo of their voices, still? Dare she evoke the past? But the past belonged to Liri, she thought sadly, and anyway, Gideon was married, now.

Yet reluctantly she was forced to admit that the little lodge would make a perfect home for an artist. An artist who lived alone, she acknowledged as she walked through the empty rooms – and provided that artist wanted to buy it. Take the large, light bedroom in which she stood, for instance. It would make a perfect studio. With windows at either end there would be good light for most of the day. And there were such views, whichever way she looked.

No sprawls of houses; no factories. Just fields and hedges and woods and the distant hills giving way to the sky. *If* this house was hers, she would probably place her bed here in the studio she considered, lips pursed; a couch against the wall maybe; a chest for her clothes and still there would be room enough for her easel and drawing-board. And downstairs she must have a sofa-bed so that Connie could visit, and odd chairs, covered in one of the prints of her own designing. Pale pink rosebuds on the bathroom walls and matching curtains, perhaps? And that claw-footed old bath must stay – and the brass taps.

She took a deep, steadying breath. She was weakening. Roz Haslington was taking over and Abbeyfield was Liri's scene. But Roz *or* Liri, *neither* was coming back to Abbeyfield. Sternly she shook the foolish thoughts from her head and allowed the bathroom rosebuds to remind her of what she had come to see; the real and *only* reason for her visit.

'I came to look at the rose hedge,' she whispered. To stand beside it just once more; to remember how she had waited there for Gideon and how he had not come. It would be easier, after that, to finally lay that ghost; easier then to say yes to James. There was still time to do it if she hurried. Quickly through the beechwood then over the paddock fence. Just a brief hullo and a brief goodbye. James wanted to marry her and she had prevaricated too long.

'Miss Haslington?'

Oh, damn, damn, *damn.*

'Up here,' Liri called. 'You – you're back early.'

'The farmer isn't in. I'd forgotten it was market day.'

'I see. Well – I– ' Oh, tell the truth, Liri, and shame the Devil! 'I – I was hoping you wouldn't be back, yet. I wanted to take a quick peep at Queen's Reach. Just for old times' sake, you know.'

'But of course. No trouble at all. It's empty, anyway.'

'Empty?'

'I told you there'd been changes,' he reminded her. 'But what about *this* little property? Have you seen enough? Do you like it?'

'Yes, I do,' she heard herself saying. 'Of course, it's early days yet, but I think I might stay the night in York and come back tomorrow for another look.'

Come back? What on earth was she talking about? Who was putting words into her mouth?

'A good idea. But you'll want to see the land first – the four acres?'

'Please, although I don't remember there being fields when Nanny lived here.'

'There wasn't. It was the builder's idea that a few acres might enhance the property. And there's Meadowsweet Lane, of course. That's the access road to Southgate, now.'

'Mmm. Y'know, that lane really *was* full of meadow-sweet,' Liri smiled dreamily. 'And there was honeysuckle, and dog roses and primroses and wild, white violets in the spring.'

'Pesticides,' the agent nodded gloomily. 'But how about the land?' Scenting a sale he waved an expansive arm, outlining the four acres. 'From the oak tree down to the beechwood,' he pointed. 'Then across to the clump of spruce and back up here, to the lodge. And I should mention that the farm has a right-of-way along Meadowsweet Lane. Unofficially, of course.'

But Liri was only half-listening. She was watching the rooks that cawed and quarrelled in the oak tree. They were building their nests high this spring, the sign of a good summer to come.

'Those fields are just about the size of the original reach,' she murmured. 'The four acres the very first Whitaker started with, all that time ago.'

But she made no attempt to explain. The agent was not interested in that Elizabethan yeoman; only in selling the little lodge at the end of Meadowsweet Lane and its two small fields.

'I'd like to see Southgate again.' She really *was* saying it, and in so firm a voice, too. 'I'll come back tomorrow – perhaps I'll take the bus and have a walk around the village first. Then if you could arrange for someone to meet me here in the afternoon?'

'No trouble at all. I'll come myself. Now, if you'd like to look at Queen's Reach?'

Liri closed the garden gate behind her, carefully pushing home the bolt as if she were securing her own property. And she *wasn't*. James was based in London and that was where her own future lay.

Her cheeks flushed pink and it was only then she had the grace to feel ashamed. Until a few moments ago she hadn't thought once about James. Not once.

The estate agent pushed open the high iron gates and Liri was standing again in the beloved gardens, looking at them through her grandfather's eyes, at a drive free of weeds, the short-cut grass beneath the trees and the newly pruned roses. Someone obviously cared, still.

'Shall we walk up to the house?' the agent murmured and Liri agreed, though it was only the gardens and the rose hedge she wanted to see and not really the old house with its crumbling plaster, its still-remembered smell of decay. She smiled at the cedar tree as if she were greeting an old friend and then, as they rounded the bend in the drive, shock hit her like a sudden, vicious slap.

'*No!*'

Queen's Reach had gone; vanished as if it had never existed. What had they done? Archaic it might have been, but to have destroyed it so wantonly —

'Who did it?' she hissed. 'Who *dared?*'

The fury of her attack startled the man at her side. 'I

did say there'd been changes.'

'When?' she demanded, anger thrashing through her.

'As – as far as I know it was about six years ago – just after old Sir Joseph died. A fire, you see. There'd been a severe frost and the hydrants were covered with packed ice, or so I believe. Old timbered houses burn like matchwood. By the time they'd run the hoses to the river, it was too late.'

'I see.' At least it has been accidental. 'And then what happened?'

'Sir Joseph's son kept most of the farmland, I understand, then sold what remained to a builder.'

Liri's heart thudded painfully and closing her eyes she willed herself not to care. But she did care, because in the space of a few seconds, a cold, uncaring hand had rubbed out the precious memories of her youth.

'Should we – er – do you still want to look, Miss Haslington? The builder is making a good job of the conversion. You might be pleasantly surprised.'

'I – yes, please.'

She walked with reluctance toward an unfamiliar building. She had been intent upon this pilgrimage, so best she should get it over with. And she was forced to admit that the builder had made a good start. Nothing remained of the old manor house, but where it had once stood lay an attractively terraced water-garden.

'Isn't that the stable-block?' Liri frowned, pointing ahead. 'Is that what is being converted?' Oh, why hadn't she read the brochure?

'It *is* the stable-block,' the agent smiled eagerly, 'and no expense being spared, I believe. Are you interested?'

'Oh, no.' ' He was joking,, of course, but Liri shook her head firmly. For one thing it would be far too expensive and for another it would hold too many memories. Above those stables had been a hayloft and not for anything could she live in a house where always there would be the imagined scent of newcut hay to remind her. 'I really wanted to see the rose hedge. My grandfather planted it when I was little, you see. It's between the stableyard and the paddock. It bloomed so thickly, and the lilies – you'd never believe their scent. I'll show you,' she whispered eagerly, beckoning him to follow.

The stableyard had hardly changed at all – thank heaven they'd left the cobbles – and even as she looked at it, the newly-painted stable clock chimed three times.

She stood enchanted as time stepped backward. The granite drinking-trough was still there and the old iron pump and the mounting-block. Then she half-glanced to her left, silently begging it to have been spared. And it had! Grandpa's rose hedge grew tall and sturdy, unharmed by the fire. Its leaf buds were swelling and beneath it, tiny shoots of lily of the valley peeped half an inch high.

'Grandpa's *liriconfancies*,' Liri murmured. 'He always used the old-fashioned names for flowers, you know.'

And no matter what Sir Joseph had said, he wouldn't allow a rose in that garden if it wasn't scented. Only moss roses, she recalled, and the big, blowzy Bourbons.

Liri closed her eyes, silently calling out the ghost.

'I waited for you here, Gideon, but you didn't come. And now I'm going to marry James. Soon he'll ask me again and this time I must say yes. I wanted you to know my darling . . . .'

And tomorrow morning she would look at Pond Cottage then go to the churchyard. She would say goodbye to Gran and Grandpa then return to London. She was getting ideas about Southgate Lodge and appealing though it was, her feelings would be constantly under attack if she lived there. The Whitakers had gone and a fire had destroyed the old house but another Queen's Reach was taking shape; a house which would be equally evocative. In Abbeyfield she would never be completely free of the past, but in London she would feel safer and if – *when* – she was married, she would forget. She really would.

She wasn't, she supposed, being entirely fair to James, but that quarrel was his fault, Liri sighed. There had been a party to celebrate her award – the most promising young designer of the year they'd called her – and someone breathlessly asked, 'Are you *really* going to marry the brilliant Roz, James?'

'No! Roz is going to marry *me*,' he'd flung.

James Howard was an established actor when Rosamund Haslington was making her first uncertain drawing, Liri sighed, yet his remark had unnerved her and maybe there was a grain of truth in what Connie had said. Perhaps coming to Abbeyfield really was a way of getting even with James, of doing something he didn't know about or approve of. And now she had made her protest the quarrel could be forgotten, she supposed.

She smiled at the estate agent. 'Sorry – I was miles away,' she whispered. 'I'm afraid it brought things back a bit.' Then she squared her shoulders and tilted her chin. 'Thanks,' she smiled. 'Shall we go, now?'

Later that night Liri phoned Connie from her hotel room.

'Just to let you know I'm staying the night and that I'm quite safe,' she teased.

'I was expecting it to be James again,' Connie grumbled. 'He's phoned three times already and he isn't a bit pleased. I wish you'd told him you were going away.'

Connie didn't care for James. Only when he acted – she gave him full credit for that. James didn't care for Connie, either.

'Why you stick with her in that flat when you can afford a place of your own is a mystery to me,' he constantly complained.

'I like being with Con,' Liri had defended. 'I owe her a lot.'

She remembered their first meeting. Fresh from art school, near-penniless and looking for a bed for the night, luck had taken her to the craft shop in one of the Covent Garden arcades.

'I don't suppose you'd care to buy any of these?'

She offered her portfolio and the owner of the shop had looked critically at the flower-pictures.

'They're not bad at all,' she pronounced. 'Do you want me to buy them or sell them for you on a commission basis?'

'I – I don't know,' Liri faltered. 'Which ever suits you best. I'm down here looking for work and it's more expensive than I'd thought, in London.'

'You're a bit naive, aren't you? Businesswise, I mean. Come into the back and we'll have a coffee. And the name's Connie Davies, by the way.' The firmness of her handshake was comforting and before long she had agreed to sell Liri's pictures and offered her a bed for a couple of nights.

And that temporary couple of nights became a permanent understanding and now, when Liri was establishing herself in textile design, she still stayed on in Connie's flat. After all, sooner or later she would be moving into James's place; when they were married, that was.

She wasn't liberated enough to do it without a wedding ring; Gran's old-fashioned upbringing had taken care of that. Besides, she liked Connie and looked on her as a sister, almost, and very precious to someone like herself who hadn't a living soul to call her own. Except James, of course.

'I'll be back the day after tomorrow, Con. I'm enjoying the break.'

'And you haven't bought the delightful property in

beautiful countryside?

'N-no. I never intended to. But it's lovely. I wish you could see it, Con.'

'Oh, no! Here we go!'

'Truly, I'm *not* buying it. But you'd love Abbeyfield. You really would.'

'Well – as long as you've laid that ghost . . . .'

'There isn't a ghost to lay,' Liri protested. 'You're getting as bad as James.'

'OK. Point taken. But don't go all nostalgic and let yourself get sidetracked? Have a good think, first?'

'There's nothing to think about. *I'm not buying it. I know what I'm doing.*'

But that was the trouble, Liri thought as she lay wide-eyed and restless that night. She *did* want to buy Southgate Lodge and she *didn't* know what she was doing. Not any longer.

At midnight she decided not to return to Abbeyfield in the morning, not even for one last look, but at one o'clock she had convinced herself that to come this far and not even say goodbye to Gran and Grandpa would be downright wicked.

At two o'clock she was wondering what they would accept for Southgate. She could afford it, she supposed, if she could be sure of selling the four acres. And it would be a distinct advantage to live in the north; much nearer the mills, now that she worked freelance. Besides, she wasn't at all sure about James. Sometimes, she considered, he was *too* near; sometimes he overpowered her, almost.

By the time the hands of the clock pointed to three she was mercifully asleep, but only to dream of Gideon who wasn't married after all and who had spent the past eight years searching the world for her.

The alarm shrilled her awake at eight and she felt cross and tired and bitterly disappointed. But she caught the eleven o'clock bus to Abbeyfield, in spite of her uncertainty.

'You're out of your tiny mind, Liri Haslington,' she admonished fiercely. 'This whole thing is getting out of hand!'

But last night in her dreams Gideon had kissed her so now there really was a ghost to lay. And laid it must be, because only then could she return to London, and marry James.

Liri left the bus on the outskirts of the village and walked slowly toward the churchyard, making her way carefully to the graveside.

She had never been able to feel sorrow there. Loneliness perhaps, but never grief. They were together the way they wanted to be.

Gran and Grandpa had died within six months of each other; the one of a sudden illness, the other of heartbreak.

'I've come to say goodbye,' Liri whispered with her heart. 'Don't worry about me. I'm fine. And your garden's fine, too, Grandpa. The *liriconfancies* are just showing through; thought I'd let you know.' She sighed, then turned abruptly away. *No tears, Liri. Gran could never abide tears. Smile, now.*

And she was still smiling as she walked past Queen's Reach gates and the top of Meadowsweet Lane. Now she would take a last look at Pond Cottage. Not far to go. On to the first turning, then over the stile to the footpath that led to Keeper's Cottage and the little house beside it; the house in which she had grown up.

She wanted nothing to have changed, for the memories she took away with her to be happy ones, but almost at once she knew she had set her hopes too high. She saw the sign ahead of her and sensed change already.

The stile had gone; the footpath had disappeared beneath a concrete road and the ornately-painted sign announced that Keeper's Lodge Farm was the home of the

Abbeyfield Herd of Pedigree Hereford Cattle. And to fan the flame of her disbelief, there, not twenty yards down the road hung a sturdy white gate, and painted on it the words, *Strictly Private. No Admittance.*

Angrily, Liri climbed it. Someone was taking liberties! The path to Pond Cottage had always been a right-of-way. How dare this Pedigree Hereford man make so free with a public footpath? A right-of-way was a right-of-way. It always was and always would be. She was surprised the village had countenanced its closing. It would never have happened in Sir Joseph's time, Liri thought crossly. People were becoming soft!

She stopped, searching for the pond where waterhens nested and yellow kingcups once grew thickly, but it too had disappeared. Pond Cottage had virtually gone, too; merged with Keeper's to make one large and obviously modernized farmhouse. And Pond Cottage orchard had vanished as if it had never been, its enclosing hedge torn out, its trees uprooted.

Liri remembered the Victoria plums and the Bramley apple trees, then glared at the new brick buildings which stood in their place.

'Vandal!' she choked, and turning swiftly, climbed the gate again. So much for memories, she mourned, hurt twisting inside her. Those cottages had been such pretty little places. Why did people find such pleasure in wanton change?

'If *I* bought Southgate,' she whispered, 'I wouldn't let a thing be changed. I'd sow wild-flower seeds in the lane and plant honeysuckle again. And there'd be no more pesticides allowed, if Meadowsweet Lane belonged to me. If I owned —'

What had the agent said? Something about the farm having right-of-way along that lane? *Unofficially,* hadn't he said?

'If Southgate Lodge were mine, I wouldn't give access to

Keeper's Lodge Farm, she thought waspishly. No more right-of-way, I'd tell him!'

She wished with all her heart it was within her power to deny him the privilege. How marvellous to be able to tell That Man to keep his cows out of *her* lane. What superb rough justice, she sighed.

She leaned dejectedly against the gate, watching with interest as a transporter manoeuvred into the concrete road. It was new and white with *Abbeyfield Pedigree Herefords* painted on the side. In country fashion she opened the gate to let it through; after all, she had no quarrel with the driver.

He nodded his thanks and Liri took in his white coat with APH picked out on the pocket. My, but Pedigree Hereford was a high-flyer and no mistake. Probably very rich, too. And money brought power with it. People like Pedigree Hereford closed public footpaths and drained ponds and cut down plum trees and no one lifted a finger to stop them.

Sick inside her, Liri headed for Southgate Lodge. She wasn't buying it, really she wasn't, but she must meet the agent there as they had arranged, she supposed. And there was no harm in having another look?

'Oh, but I'd like to tell That Man a thing or two!' She kicked an unoffending stone and sent it skimming along the road. 'He wouldn't get all his own way with *me.*'

The estate agent arrived just two minutes after Liri and apologised for being late.

'It doesn't matter Mr – er?'

How rude he must think her. He had introduced himself yesterday and she had not properly heard. Nor had she been sufficiently interested to ask him to repeat it. But now – just in case – it might be an advantage to know.

'Butterworth,' he supplied. 'Of Armstrong and Butterworth.'

Liri liked him a little better and favoured him with a genuine smile.

'I'd just like to wander, if you don't mind,' she murmured. 'I want to know if it's possible to see those new farm buildings from the upstairs windows. I won't be long. Wait in the car, if you'd like?'

Strangely apprehensive, she looked at the kitchen again and the large, light living-room, loving it and all its memories. Abbeyfield was cheating, she sighed, recognising her, claiming her back.

Reluctantly she climbed the stairs and stood at the bedroom window. It was all right. The beechwood screened the brash brick cowsheds. When the trees came into leaf, she would not be able to see them at all; nor the tarted-up farmhouse that had gobbled up Pond Cottage.

Not that it mattered, she sighed. Even allowing for the extra work the award was bringing, she was still a freelance and could be feasting one week and fasting the next.

She focused her gaze on the distant wisp of smoke that trailed from the chimney of Woodsman's Cottage. But couldn't the bank make her a loan? Didn't just about everybody have an overdraft, these days? And there were the flower-pictures, too. Connie could sell all she could paint – she'd said so.

Liri took a last glance around the room that would have made such a perfect studio. She was going to marry James, wasn't she? She must not allow herself such silly daydreams.

Quietly and finally she turned her back, and closing the front door behind her walked slowly through the garden to gaze over the hawthorn hedge at the two small fields.

There was always the land, of course. It would bring quite a lot of money if someone wanted it badly enough.

But she could never sell it, she realized. She couldn't bear it if those four acres ended up as part of Keeper's Lodge Farm.

But *if* she bought Southgate Lodge she could at least deny Pedigree Hereford the use of Meadowsweet Lane, she realized with elation. Even things up for the destruction of Pond Cottage!

'Liri Haslington, what *are* you thinking about?' she gasped.

She couldn't buy a house merely to get even with a man she had never met. It was thoroughly childish and very bad business and if Connie could read her thoughts right now she would blow her top.

No, thought Liri, *if* she bought the little lodge it would be because she loved it and not because it had once been a part of another life. And she would want it because it brought her nearer to Gran and Grandpa and if she couldn't go back to Pond Cottage then wouldn't Southgate be the next best thing? And it was such a comforting little house, vibrating with warmth and welcome.

Oh, Grandpa. What am I to do?

And that was the precise moment at which Mr Butterworth chose to appear on the other side of the hedge.

'Hullo, there. Any snags?'

'None, that I can see,' she smiled.

What was she saying? But it was Grandpa's fault. He'd made the estate agent appear at exactly the right time and in exactly the right place. He couldn't have chosen a better time or a sneakier place.

Liri closed her eyes and saw glowing coals, chintz-covered chairs and a long brass toasting-fork hanging beside the fireplace and thought back to the innocent days before love had flamed.

'I could wrap that innocence around me,' she thought. 'I would be safe, then. Safe from James who wants me and safe from Gideon, who did not.'

'You like it?'

Liri tilted her chin and sent her thoughts winging across the four acres and high over the beechwood. She hoped That Man would get the message, because it was going out loud and clear.

Oh, but you're in for a shock, my high-flying friend!

Just wait until he saw that gate at the top of Meadowsweet Lane; that large white gate, exactly like the one which blocked the road to Pond Cottage; that *magnificent* gate on which would be painted *Strictly Private. No Admission.*

'Miss Haslington?'

'Oh – er – like it? Yes, I do,' she gasped. 'I like it very much indeed.'

Dear heaven, what was she saying? She had taken leave of her senses. She really had.

'Then if we can agree on a price, Miss Haslington?'

'And if the surveyor's report isn't too alarming, Mr Butterworth.'

Liri closed her eyes and swallowed hard.

'Did you hear that, Grandpa?' she whispered inside her. 'D'you know, I think I've just bought a house.'

Two

Liri was dismayed to see James at the barrier when she arrived at King's Cross.

'How did you know which train I'd be on?' she faltered, lifting her cheek to be kissed.

'Connie told me eventually you'd be back this morning. I had to make a guess at the time.'

'Connie didn't know for certain,' Liri defended. 'I didn't know myself.'

'You could have phoned.'

'But you're always at the theatre, nights.'

'I invariably work evenings. It's my profession, sweetie.' James was piqued. 'Hadn't you thought of ringing in the afternoon or do I only rate off-peak calls? I don't understand you sometimes, Roz. And why Yorkshire?'

'Why not? It's home, isn't it?'

'Your home is where I am – or *should* be,' he frowned, taking her elbow. 'Better hurry. I'm awkwardly parked.'

James with a parking ticket was not the nicest of

persons, and Liri hurried. Nor did she speak again until
he demanded, 'Tell me Roz – why this sudden longing for
your native heath?' He was *very* piqued.

They were clear of the station now, with James
impatiently nosing his car into the traffic.

'I – well, there was a house for sale in the Sunday paper
– a house I knew. It must have reminded me, I suppose.'

'So you go tearing off without so much as a word?' He
glared at her as if she alone was responsible for the
crawling queue they had just become a part of. 'Just to
see a house? Well, I hope you got your money's worth?'

'No.' Her mouth was suddenly dry. 'It had gone; burned
down and a garden in its place. You'd never have known
Queen's Reach had ever existed. But *I* knew.' She
stopped to draw breath. Why was he making her so
nervous? 'There was another house, though. It had once
been the stables. And Pond Cottage was —'

'The lady doth protest too much, methinks,' James's
voice was thick with sarcasm. 'What have you *really* been
up to, darling?'

Liri closed her eyes and began to count. James was
right. She even sounded guilty. In a flat voice she
whispered, 'Don't throw your Shakespeare at *me*.' She
was learning that the best defence against James's
arrogance was to attack it, head on. 'And don't demand to
know what I've been doing. We're not married, yet.'

She clenched her hands tightly. They mustn't quarrel.
Quarrelling upset her more than he realized. It affected
her work, too. After a clash with James her mind refused
to function.

'Sorry, darling, but you did leave me in the dark. Might
I *ask* if you had an enjoyable time?'

'You might James and I did, thank you.'

'You'd see old friends, I suppose?'

'I didn't as a matter of fact. The only person I spoke to
was the estate agent. It's a long time since I left

Abbeyfield. Things change.'

The traffic was moving again and James accelerated fiercely and changed lanes. Liri drew in her breath and slammed a foot on an imaginary brake.

'No old flames?'

'No. But I was furious with Pedigree Hereford.'

'*Who?*'

'Oh, I don't know his name, but he breeds Herefords – cattle, you know. He's knocked Pond Cottage and Keeper's Lodge into one and torn out our orchard. And he's put a gate across a right-of-way.'

'Gad, ma'am. The fellow's a bounder!'

'It's not funny, James. Not in the country.' Then she smiled, thankful the tension between them had lessened. 'How's the play going?' James liked to talk about his work.

'Very well indeed. Pity we could only get the theatre for a short run. I was talking to Bennett Saunders yesterday.'

'The playwright?'

'The same. He's had a television series commissioned and I've an idea I was being sounded out. Did you eat on the train, by the way?'

'No. I wasn't hungry.'

'Come back to my place then and I'll fix you an omelette.'

James was good at omelettes. Liri supposed he'd be good at making love, too. Strange they should be hovering on the brink of marriage yet they had never been lovers. They almost had, many times yet she always managed to cry off. Always me, Liri admitted. It was the cause of most of their quarrels. It was the reason she stayed on with Connie, truth known.

'Penny for them, Roz?'

'I was thinking about your omelettes,' she lied. She hadn't planned on having lunch with James. She was only accepting because she felt a sudden rush of guilt about Yorkshire. 'Sounds a good idea.'

When Liri got back to the flat, Connie was heating a tin of soup.

'Hi,' she said, without looking up. 'Hungry?'

Liri shook her head. 'I had a late lunch with James. He's gone to the theatre early tonight, thank goodness, to go through a piece they're changing in the second act.'

'I'll give the devil his due, he works hard,' Connie grinned. 'But why *thank goodness?* Not another row?'

'No, but I was glad to get away. I felt all strung up and James can read me like a book. I wanted to talk to you about it first. I'm thinking very seriously about buying Southgate Lodge, you see. I – I've arranged to have it surveyed.' The words tumbled out. 'Oh, Connie, don't say I can't afford it?'

'Why should I? I don't know yet what they're asking for it. And there's nothing wrong in having a house surveyed – just as long as you haven't signed anything.'

'Of course I haven't. But it's perfect. You know what those little gate-lodges are like – all quaint and pretty on the outside? There were three of them once, but Southgate's the only one left, now. And Queen's Reach has gone, too. But take a look at this, Con.' Hurriedly she took the brochure from her handbag, her eyes anxious. 'Read it, then you'll see what I mean.'

'You really want it, don't you?' Connie murmured eventually. 'Is it as nice as it sounds?'

'Nicer. The views are marvellous. And Con, you *do* like it!'

'Sounds ideal for a career person living alone and when you've sold that land —'

'No! I couldn't let the land go.'

'Why ever not?'

'W-e-ell, if I put them on the market, those four acres could get into the wrong hands. There's this farmer, you see. It's a feeling I've got about him.'

She told Connie about Pedigree Hereford, then, and about Pond Cottage orchard and the new concrete road. It poured out in a deluge of indignation.

'Hey! Hold on and listen.' Connie held up a commanding hand. 'You're doing quite well, careerwise, and I'm in favour of your investing some of your earnings in a place of your own. But don't you think you're being a bit unreasonable? Those fields could be worth about half as much as the house itself, I shouldn't wonder. You just can't tie up money in land you've no use for; land you seem determined no one else is going to use, either. But there's more to this than meets the eye, isn't there? A man, for instance?'

'Yes. Gideon Whitaker.' It came out without a second's hesitation and oh, the joy of saying his name; the sweet, blessed relief of it. 'It was a long time ago, but I was very much in love with him. And you needn't look so disapproving; he's married now.'

'Is he indeed? Then take my advice and forget that little house. Keep away, or you'll be sorry, I guarantee it.'

'Don't worry,' Liri shook her head impatiently. 'He's not there now. The estate has been sold off and the family's all gone. It's just that seeing Abbeyfield again brought it all back.'

'And now you fancy doing a Miss Havisham? You want to sit there like something out of Dickens, mourning your lost love?'

'Of course not. But I've realized I can't marry James – not yet, anyway. I'll have to get right away for a time so I might as well go back to Abbeyfield as go anywhere.'

'You really mean it, don't you, Roz?'

'Yes,' Liri nodded fiercely. 'I can work just as easily there as I can here. I don't just want Southgate Lodge. I *need* it.'

'I think,' said Connie grimly, 'we'd better have a drink.'

'Think we better had,' Liri choked, 'and make mine a big one. I'm so mixed up I feel like getting plastered. Either that, or crying my eyes out. I want to stay here, yet I want to go home.'

'Y'know, there's still the surveyor,' Connie ruminated, handing Liri a glass. 'He just might save your bacon. With luck he'll find dry rot and damp and woodworm in the roof. Or there might even be a motorway planned, right through the middle of it. Now that would take care of it, once and for all.'

'I suppose it would,' Liri whispered.

But there would still be all the newly awakened memories. Who would take care of them?

'That surveyor,' Connie Davies frowned when the eagerly awaited report arrived, 'is a dratted nuisance. Seems there's nothing much wrong with the place.'

'Looks like it.' Liri's heart thumped excitedly. 'What do you think about his valuation?'

'Reasonable. But in your case, a lot too much. If only you'd be sensible, Roz; at least consider selling those fields.'

'I don't want to. I – I *can't*.'

'Exactly. So in my opinion, you should forget the whole thing.'

'I want Southgate Lodge,' Liri muttered.

'All right – so lease out the land? That way you'd be getting some return for your money.'

'Why must everything revolve around money?' Liri flung.

'Because that's the way life is, lovey. And it's downright immoral to let good land lay idle,' Connie clucked. 'All this fuss, just because some fool of a farmer pulled up an orchard and put a gate across a right-of-way. I thought you had more sense, Roz.'

'Then it seems I haven't, doesn't it? And don't ask me to explain, because I can't. I just feel I must go back. It's as if something's pulling me. It's like the whole thing has been taken out of my hands.'

'In that case, you'd better have a word with the bank if your mind's made up.'

'You *do* approve, Con!' Liri gasped. 'You just won't admit it, that's all.'

'I *don't* approve, but at least I know when I'm beaten. Go on. Ring the bank . . . .'

Liri handed over the brochure and the surveyor's report and the bank manager, when he had read them, actually smiled.

'Quite a nice little property, Miss Haslington, and the land appears to be in good heart. But you'll be selling that – or part of it?'

Oh why, why, *why* did everything have to depend upon those four acres?

'Of course. I don't think I'll have any difficulty in that direction.' It slipped out so easily she shocked herself.

Never lie to your priest, your doctor or your bank manager, someone once said. Liri couldn't remember who, exactly, but it was someone who didn't care about rights-of-way, or ponds, or poor, uprooted orchards; someone who had never loved Gideon.

'Well then, I wish you luck. But go carefully? Offer a little less.' He blinked at her over the top of his glasses. 'Let me know how it goes?'

Liri flashed him a smile and assured him she would.

She had no idea why she took a taxi back to the flat. She felt so elated she could have flown there. For just a minute she hesitated, then taking in a deep, calming breath, she lifted the phone and dialled the York number.

Mr Butterworth was having lunch with a client, his secretary told Liri and Mr Armstrong was out on a survey. Could she perhaps ring again? After three?

Dismayed, Liri replaced the receiver. She had not expected snags. Three o'clock was almost two hours away. She could work, she supposed, or even wash her hair? But work was out of the question and her hair was shining clean so instead she walked to the local shops and bought a long brass toasting-fork.

'For Southgate Lodge,' she muttered. 'To bring me luck.'

Exactly at three o'clock she phoned Mr Butterworth again. At five minutes past she was sitting stunned, refusing to believe a word of it.

'I'm really sorry, Miss Haslington. But this morning I had an offer from another party – considerably in excess of yours, I'm afraid,' the estate agent sighed.

'How much more?' Liri choked.

How could she have been so stupid as to imagine no one else but herself was interested in the little lodge?

'Well, if you raise your offer another five thousand pounds, say?'

Five *thousand?*

'It's a question of the land, I fear,' the voice droned on. 'The other party is principally interested in that, you see.'

'I – I'll think about it,' Liri whispered. 'I'll ring you back tomorrow.'

'I can't wait much longer, I'm afraid. You'll appreciate my position?'

Yes, she did. She really did. She closed her eyes tightly to stop the tears. She had been so sure, yet now they were asking for an outrageous £5,000 *more*.

But it could only be Pedigree Hereford and his dirty-tricks department, she raged silently. He'd get Meadowsweet Lane, too, and now she would never plant violets there, nor honeysuckle, nor wild white roses.

Head in hands she began to sob. She was still red-eyed and sniffy when her flat-mate got home.

'Five thousand?' she jerked derisively. 'Well that settles it. Forget it, love.' She hugged Liri tightly. 'There'll be other houses.'

But never another little house in Abbeyfield; never another Southgate Lodge, Liri thought. Not in a million years.

Next morning, James sent roses. It was uncanny, Liri thought. It was as if he sensed she had just taken a beating and was pressing his advantage while she was still reeling.

That same afternoon, he called. Liri saw his car in the street below and refused to answer his knock. She didn't want to talk to him yet. She was really trying to forget the Abbeyfield affair as it was now called. She and Connie had even had words about it or rather Connie had. Banging her fist on the table-top she issued an ultimatum.

'Now listen, Roz! This Abbeyfield affair is getting out of hand. I'm becoming tired of your moods. Yes, *moods*,' she asserted when Liri opened her mouth to protest. 'You're acting like a spoiled brat!'

'Not you, too?' Liri gasped. 'You tell me to invest my savings sensibly, then when I try to I'm told to forget it. I really wanted Southgate.'

'Now hold on, love. We do business together and I'm your friend, I hope, but I don't *tell* you anything. However, I don't think now that the house in Yorkshire would have been a good investment. All that hard-earned money, tied up in a few acres of hallowed land?'

Liri closed her eyes. Connie was right. Drat her, she was always right.

How she wished she had stayed away from Abbeyfield, she mourned silently. Maybe she should never have left it, truth known, but having, done so, she should never have gone back.

But it aggravated her to think that Pedigree Hereford was getting the land because it *was* him, she was sure of it. He'd be getting the original reach; the four acres given to that very first Whitaker all those years ago and if no one else cared about it, then she *did,* Liri thought passionately.

But £5,000 more was out of the question. And she wasn't acting like a spoiled child, although Connie could be forgiven for thinking she was.

She lifted the curtain and watched James drive away then sat at her drawing-board, chin on hands. Connie understood her so well, Liri admitted. It was the only thing she didn't approve of in her flat-mate. Not only was she always right, she was clairvoyant, too.

But when Connie got home that evening she looked with approval at Liri's sketches.

'That's the ticket. Back in business again?'

'Mm. Just trying out a few ideas for next spring, though I'm not too sure about colours. I was thinking about yellows and greens and white, maybe.'

Primroses and daffodils and the innocent green of unfolding beech leaves. And what about a rose and lily-of-the-valley design and oh, Abbeyfield, why are you tormenting me so?

'Afraid I'm not very bright when it comes to forward trends. But I'm getting low on flower pictures – how about doing me one or two of those? If you've nothing more urgent, that is?'

'I haven't,' Liri whispered. 'Don't worry, Con. The Abbeyfield affair is over. And just to prove it,' she said brightly, 'I'll make the supper while you put your feet up and have a look at what I've been doing.'

And she had got over it, she really had. But if only it wasn't such a dear little house she sighed, and so very precious with memories.

Liri dabbed dry the lettuce and arranged it on a dish. Lettuce-washing was one of her least favourite things, she reflected. Lettuce-washing, letter-writing and lovers but not necessarily in that order.

Take lovers, for instance. Old loves, new loves. Gideon was married, but James was not. And James was becoming impatient, she admitted, deliberately turning her thoughts to the tomatoes and the shocking price she had paid for them.

Now Grandpa's tomatoes had been wonderful, hanging in heavy scarlet trusses, warm from the sun with the smell of the greenhouse on them and – oh, damn, damn, damn! *Why* had she gone back to Abbeyfield, and just as she had been on the point of saying yes to James?

Yes to marriage, had it been, or yes to lovemaking?

Topping and tailing the spring onions, she dropped them into water. Onions. If James called tonight on his way to the theatre her kiss would be sharp with the tang of them, she thought defiantly.

'Cheese for afters, or fruit?' she called.

'Mmmm . . . .'

Liri laid both on the table. 'Ready in one minute,' she warned.

'Well?' she demanded when Connie laid down the sketches and drew up a chair. 'Anything there that looks promising?' Deftly she halved the pizza.

'They're all fine. You're good at flowers.'

'I was brought up with them,' Liri smiled, taking another onion.

If only she could order her life as she ordered her career. She was a grown woman and if James was to be believed, an attractive one. Yet since the Abbeyfield affair she had never been so unsure or so desperately unhappy; at least not since the night she left Pond Cottage's keys at the estate office and walked away from Queen's Reach for ever.

'James came today,' she murmured.

Connie lifted an eyebrow, but made no comment.

'I – I pretended not to be in. Well, I was busy,' she defended.

'Of course. And you're going to be so busy that one morning you'll open the paper and see a smiling James Howard and his heiress bride.'

'I thought you didn't care for James,' Liri pouted.

'Let's say I can take him or leave him,' Connie shrugged. 'But in your case it's not that simple. The man's in love with you and you're going to have to make up your mind, Roz. You defend your virginity like —'

'I'm – I'm not a virgin.' Liri took an apple and sliced it laboriously.

'Oh? You could have fooled me.'

'It was a long time ago. Do I have to spell it out, Con?'

'I think you'd better. Abbeyfield, wasn't it?'

Liri nodded dumbly.

'Go on, then.'

'Like I said, Con, I was in love with Gideon Whitaker.'

'The squire's son?' the other woman pressed relentlessly.

'*Second* son. There's a world of difference. Matthew was the elder brother. It seems that after Sir Joseph died there was a fire and Matthew sold out and left.'

'And the other one?'

'Gideon had already gone to Canada.'

'I see. He loved you and left you?'

'Something like that,' Liri choked. 'You know the rest.'

'No, I don't.' Connie's voice was quiet and even, her no-nonsense voice. 'Come to think of it, I've known you for more than five years and parts of you are still a mystery to me.'

'All right, then. Maybe you'd better know.' Liri flared. 'Help you to understand the other me, the person behind Rosamund Haslington B.A. I'm a love-child, Con,

although there's another less attractive name now for
people like me. My mother left me at Pond Cottage with
my grandparents and went to America, looking for my
foot-loose Daddy! She found him *and* his wife, then got
sick and died over there in a charity hospital run by
nuns.'

'So? Tragic, I'll admit, but it wasn't your fault.'

'No. I suppose not. It was a nine-days' wonder in
Abbeyfield, I believe, then people forgot. I'd got around to
thinking it didn't matter.'

'But it did?'

'Seems so. We wanted to be married, Gideon and I.
We'd decided to tell our folks – first Sir Joseph, then
Grandpa. We decided that if they made a fuss we'd do it
anyway, as soon as I was eighteen.' She speared a piece
of apple and regarded it gravely. 'But we didn't, and
that's it . . .'

'No, Roz. There's more to it than that. Something
happened to turn you into an ice maiden,' Connie said
flatly. 'I shouldn't wonder if you weren't quite human,
once.'

'All right, so he *jilted* me. Lovely old-fashioned word,
isn't it?' Liri flung. 'The night we were going to bring it
out into the open, I waited for him. I waited hours, but he
never came. In the end Grandpa told me. Gone to
Canada, he said. I couldn't believe it. I wouldn't. Gideon
must have known he was going – everyone must've
known, but me.'

And two years later, she brooded, in the waiting-room of
a Liverpool dentist, she finally stopped loving him. In a
society glossy, she read of his engagement and banished
him from her life. Or so she had thought.

'I didn't think things like that happened any more,'
Connie said, eventually.

'Oh, but they do – *did* – in Abbeyfield,' Liri whispered.

'So you vowed you'd show the lot of them, uh?'

'Not exactly, but it turned out that way. Not long after, Grandpa died. Influenza, they said, but it turned to pneumonia. It was a terrible shock. Gran just seemed to opt out of the world. She died six months after for no reason at all. Heartbreak, I suppose, only they say there's no such thing . . . .'

Her voice trailed away, but if she expected sympathy, none came.

'And then what?' came the ruthless demand.

'The rest you know. I decided to take up art, as Gran always wanted me to do. So I got a place at Liverpool Polytechnic; sold everything in Pond Cottage and handed the key in at the estate office. I just walked away and told no one where I was going. I was bitter. I hadn't intended going back – ever.'

'But you made good and you were determined to show them? Can't say I blame you.'

'No, Con. It didn't start out like that. Liri didn't want to do that. She only wanted to say goodbye to the past. Liri wouldn't have —'

'*Liri?*'

'That's me. My other self. Liri was my pet-name as a child. But it was Roz Haslington who had all the ambition. After Liri discovered that Gideon was engaged, Roz took over completely and worked like a fiend to get a degree.'

'You don't half complicate things, old love. I suppose that whenever James gets ardent it's this Liri person freezing him out?'

'If you want to go all Freudian – yes, I suppose it is.'

'Hm. I could almost feel sorry for the man. You're not only attractive, Roz, you're also completely inaccessible. To someone like James, that's a real challenge.'

'I know. And the answer's simple, really. All I have to do is let him make love to me – just once. He'd lose interest then. I sometimes think it's what I want to happen, deep down.'

'Flaming Norah! I wish you'd never read that advert. You go poking about, resurrecting old loves – oh, what's the use?' Connie shrugged. 'It's your life I suppose, but I wish you'd put the Abbeyfield affair behind you. You're doing well. Your career's taken off and an actor that half the females in this country wouldn't say no to wants to marry you. Don't let the past stand in your way. Had you thought, Roz, you could pass that Gideon fellow in the street and never know it? He's probably got a receding hairline and a paunch, now. Settle for James and half a loaf. Or be a contented spinster like me and give up bread altogether.'

'Very clever, Miss Davies, and like always, I'm prepared to take your advice.'

'Good. So get on with *today*. The past is done Roz, and so has that soft-hearted kid called Liri. And Southgate Lodge has gone, too. You tried, but someone has beaten you to it. You weren't intended to go back to Abbeyfield or to meet Gideon Whitaker again. Accept it?'

'I'll try, and as usual you're right, Con. As a matter of fact it's the one thing about you I can't stand. You're *always* right,' Liri grimaced. 'And as from now the Abbeyfield affair is taboo, I promise. Completely forgotten.'

But such statements, Liri was to find next morning, have a nasty habit of back-firing.

At exactly half-past ten, when the rose and lily design was beginning to take shape nicely, the phone at her elbow shattered her newly found tranquillity.

'Miss Haslington? Good morning.' There was no mistaking the unexpected voice.

'Mr Butterworth! How's York?'

She knew what he was going to say and she didn't want

him to say it. Not now. Not when she was prepared to settle for half a loaf.

'It's fine, as always. But I'm ringing about Southgate Lodge. You'll be pleased to know that the other party – er –'

'The man who offered five thousand pounds more?' Her lips were so stiff it was hard to say the words.

'Exactly. Well, this morning he withdrew his offer. And gave no explanation, either. Most upsetting.'

'So it's on the market again?'

Fool, Liri! Tell him your offer is withdrawn, too!

'It is.'

'I'm sorry, Mr Butterworth, but I'm not prepared to go any higher.'

That's it. Be firm.

'Ah, yes. As a matter of fact, I've just had a word with the vendor. He would consider your original offer, I'm almost sure.'

Oh, why had this happened? Liri yearned. And she had wanted Southgate Lodge so much and the four acres, *and* a sturdy white gate at the top of Meadowsweet Lane.

'Could we arrange another meeting, Miss Haslington?'

'I'm very busy, Mr Butterworth.'

She couldn't go to Abbeyfield again. She dare not!

'Mr Masters – he's the vendor – will be in London on Monday. I'm sure he'd be willing to discuss the matter with you over lunch.'

'I'm – I'm not at all sure I can make it.'

It was her last feeble stand and she knew she would weaken, and yield. She had wanted Southgate Lodge as soon as she saw it, and nothing, absolutely nothing, had changed.

Sunday was James's day of rest, the one day on which Liri could be sure he would appear. After midday, hopefully, when he would have caught up on his sleep and be more amenable to sudden shock; that she was again considering the purchase of the house in Yorkshire, for instance, and that she was meeting a Mr Masters the following day to allow herself to be finally persuaded. She had felt almost happy, until James arrived early, that was. He was carrying more roses and a box of her favourite mints, and James bearing gifts was always unnerving.

'Darling.' he kissed her firmly, his lips lingering warmly. He kissed so beautifully that Liri could never be certain if he was acting, or not. It was the same, too, when their loveplay began. She would listen to his words, trying to match them to lines from his plays, rather than enjoying them.

Really, though, it was her way of turning off, of making sure she was always in possession of sufficient breath with which to cry 'No!' Automatically, she pulled away.

'Where's Connie?' he smiled.

Whenever Connie was out, James's masculinity asserted itself.

'Gone to Hammersmith.'

James removed his jacket and draped it over a chair. Even a simple thing like that he did beautifully, Liri admitted grudgingly.

'Good.' He reached for her, tilting her chin, touching her lips with his. He liked her to be unresponsive for the first few kisses, then, when he had relaxed her mouth his forefinger would trace the outline of her face, exploring its highs and hollows, following the fingertip routine with his lips; kissing her closed eyelids, the hollow at her throat.

His hands would cup the rounds of her shoulders then, and slip down her arms and up again to her breasts. And that was unfair, because whenever he gentled her breasts they would respond to his touch as they were doing now.

'Don't!' she cried harshly. 'We haven't had lunch yet and —'

He took a backward step and focused his eyes on hers. Liri tried to look away, but could not. She saw his mouth, hard with need, his nostrils tight with restraint. Her heart thudded with fear. It had to be *now*. Once James had made love to her he would lose interest.

And you will forget Gideon! her heart cried.

She reached out, her eyes closed her lips parted, pressing herself closer. Now it was she who acted. Not words or movements from a play, but something far more real. Now she was calling out a ghost.

Remember, my long-ago darling? This was the way it was between us. I gave myself gladly. I wasn't cold then. I wanted you. My pounding, pulsating body wanted you. And the hay smelled sweet and oh, my dearest love —

A sob escaped her lips only to be stifled by the hardness of James's mouth. She heard his low laugh of triumph, heard the grating of a zip and felt her housecoat swish to her feet.

She clung more tightly, her head on his shoulder. She didn't want him to see her nakedness. Why hadn't he come tonight? Tonight, in the darkness, surrender would have been easier.

He pushed her a little way from him. His hands were hurting her arms, his eyes devouring her body. She had never let things get this far before, she thought wildly, and now he was savouring the moment. He had won, because now they had passed the point of no return.

Her bedsheets would be soft and smell faintly of her perfume. Not like the hay with the warmth of summer on it and its receding roughness as Gideon straddled her, pressing her down, down.

There had been chinks in the hayloft roof that let in slivers of starlight, the last thing she had seen before closing her eyes and giving herself.

James swept her into his arms, carrying her to the unmade bed.

Why did you leave me, Gideon? Why did you marry someone else when I loved you so – still love you?

'*My darling!*' James was himself, now; the acting was over.

Pretend, Liri. Pretend!

'No!' The word tore itself harshly from her throat. She struggled to her feet, tugging at the quilt, wrapping it around her nakedness. 'Leave me alone. Leave me – aaah . . . .'

'*Damn it, woman!*' He threw her to the bed again then raised his clenched fist.

Liri closed her eyes. She had led him too far and now he would strike her. And if he did it would be no more than she deserved. She closed her eyes and waited, but the blow did not fall.

'No,' she moaned. 'I can't, James. Forgive me, but I can't.'

'All right, Roz. But next time you let it go that far, I'll *take* you, so help me. Is that the way it's got to be? Is that what you want?'

She stood there shaking, retching. She heard the banging of the outside door, the slamming of his feet on the stairs.

She wanted to weep, but she could not. Tomorrow at ten she was seeing the bank manager again. Then she was meeting Mr Masters.

She was buying Southgate Lodge. It was all she must think about. Once it was hers, once she had its warmth to wrap around her, she would be capable of coherent thought again.

Icy cold she bolted the door, then loosening her grip on the quilt, walked naked to the shower.

She would wash away the touch of James's hands, make herself a strong coffee then sit at her drawing-board and forget everything until Connie returned. She would even forget Abbeyfield. Until tomorrow, that was, when she would tell Mr Masters she wanted to buy Southgate Lodge.

Strangely and suddenly the trembling ceased. Tomorrow those four precious acres would be in her keeping and no one, not Connie nor James nor even the ghost of a love that was gone, could prevent it.

She sighed, and held up her face to the warm, redeeming water.

Three

L iri stood at the window, her heart thumping with
pleasure. The willow in the garden was bursting
green, the apple tree heavy with pale pink blossom
and the sky so high and wide and blue it just wasn't
possible.

'I had forgotten,' she whispered, 'how very beautiful
April can be. And all this is mine, now. I'm home.'

She blinked hard. She wasn't going to cry. The feeling
inside her was merely one of relief that the worrying was
over; that she was really here. She would be all right
once she had become accustomed to the feeling of
homecoming, of being close to her youth again.

'And now what?' she whispered. 'Would she, dare she
make that wish? Could she risk its not coming true?
Bread-and-salt wishes were powerful things; how then
could she waste one on something so utterly impossible?

Yet perversely she had come prepared. The bread was
in her holdall and the salt, both ready to be carried from

room to room. It stood to reason, Liri frowned. Southgate
Lodge was built almost 400 years ago and many people
had lived in it and loved in it; had been born here and
died here and they couldn't have helped but leave
something of themselves behind. Surely all those years
could not wholly be lost in time? Best that the spirits still
lingering here should know she meant them no harm;
best she should make sure?

'I'm Liri,' she whispered to the memories in the empty,
echoing room. 'Perhaps you remember me? I've come to
live here.'

Without another thought she took out the bread and
salt, holding them with hands that trembled.

'Stop it!' she commanded as nostalgia ached through
her. This was no longer Nanny Brightwell's cottage and
Gideon would never come here again. It was the spirits of
the long-gone she was placating, not the memory of a lost
love.

Defiantly she tilted her chin, and salt in her left hand,
bread in her right she walked from room to room, smiling
a greeting, whispering 'Hullo.' Then firmly she walked
downstairs again and placed the bread and salt on the
living-room hearth. There they must lie all night and
tomorrow, when all would be harmony in the little house,
she would throw the bread to the birds, toss a pinch of the
salt over her shoulder, and make her wish.

'Idiot,' she chided. 'A woman of letters doing the bread-
and-salt thing like a medieval peasant.'

But wasn't she a peasant, at heart? And hadn't Gran
bread-and-salted Pond Cottage? Hadn't everyone done it,
hereabouts? Making sure could do no harm at all, and
besides, there was the wish . . . .

Spirits appeased, conscience eased, Liri filled the kettle.
First a mug of tea, then down to work and no stopping
until everything was unpacked.

Liri worked without pause and by early evening she

had made her bed in the studio upstairs, set up her drawing-board and arranged her paint pots and inks into neat rows. She looked with affection at the pine chest which was Connie's parting gift and with pride at the bed-cover and curtains of Rosamund Haslington's designing.

'I'm really here,' she whispered, hugging herself tightly. Her savings had gone and the bank owned half of Southgate, but this little house would be good to her, it *would*.

She smiled a goodnight to the beechwood, shadowy now in the half-light then gazed at the dim outline of Keeper's Lodge Farm, realizing that since the night she left Pond Cottage, this was the first time she had been truly alone. Now she was exhausted yet too excited to rest. Everything seemed to have happened so quickly after Mr Butterworth's phonecall. Thank heaven for a friend, she sighed, who had remained unflappable throughout.

Last night she and Connie had talked late, discussing everything under the sun as friends who are to part seem always to do and it was inevitable that their conversation should turn to the four acres. 'You're still determined not to sell?' Connie had asked.

'Yes,' Liri nodded.

'Lease them out, then?'

'We-ell, maybe. But there'd have to be no sub-letting, Con. *He* mustn't get his hands on them.'

'This Pedigree Hereford's got you really rattled, Roz, and you haven't even met the man.'

'I don't want to meet him. All I want now is a gate at the top of my lane.'

'But you've got your house – don't be vindictive.'

'A gate at the top of Meadowsweet Lane,' Liri repeated. 'No more right-of-way for That Man's cows.'

'Well, I can only say that your attitude surprises me.' Connie had seemed genuinely shocked. 'You can't go into a small community and start throwing your weight about the minute you set foot in the place. Even I know that. They won't like it, you know. The locals will close ranks against you.'

'They won't,' Liri retorted. '*I'm* a local. I was born there, remember? It's Pedigree Hereford who's the incomer.'

Connie had surrendered at that point, but if she had doubts about the hurried departure to darkest Yorkshire, James most certainly did not. He had continued to call regularly and on his best behaviour, too, acting with his customary charm. *Acting,* Liri had stressed silently, because James was taking the buying of Southgate much too calmly. Almost as if he knew something she did not, she frowned.

But he had made no more advances since that stormy Sunday, treating her gently, kissing her with restraint. Except once, that was. Last night he had made a brief call before going on to the theatre, his eyes narrowing as he kissed her hungrily.

'I haven't given up, Roz,' he murmured. 'You know that, don't you?'

But she should have gone through with it that Sunday, Liri realized. She should have closed her heart and her mind and allowed his lovemaking. It would all have been over now, if she had. But that kind of thing isn't done, she reminded herself, not if you love someone else – even if that someone else has completely forgotten you.

'Stop it!' she commanded sternly, and drawing the curtains against the oncoming night, walked quickly downstairs to dial Connie's number.

'Hi, there. Just thought I'd let you know everything's fine.'

'No problems?'

'None that won't be straightened out by this time tomorrow. I still can't quite believe any of it, though it's funny without you, Con.'

'I miss you, too, but I'll be up to see you very soon. And don't go starting any vendettas with Pedigree Hereford. Count up to ten, first?'

Of course she would count up to ten, Liri conceded as she replaced the receiver, and of course she wouldn't be starting any vendettas. But she still wanted the gate, she thought rebelliously. That Man's comings and goings along *her* lane would soon be at an end.

Deliberately she dismissed him from her mind. Nothing, she asserted, as she surrendered to the peace of the little house, must be allowed to spoil the magic of this day. Everything was so still that she could almost touch the silence. Across the fields, *her* fields, the lights of Keeper's Lodge Farm shone brightly and beyond them a mellow light glowed in an upstairs window of Woodsman's Cottage.

It was all so beautiful and unbelievable and she closed her eyes tightly.

'I'm back,' she whispered to the litter of boxes and cases and crumpled paper. 'I'm really home again,' and taking the brass toasting-fork she had purchased so hopefully, hung it beside the fireplace.

Funny, she thought, that the hook should still be there . . . .

Liri awoke to the ringing of the telephone and stumbled downstairs to answer it. 'Where on earth . . . ?' she grumbled, and flopping to her knees, picked up the receiver.

'Lo,' she mumbled sleepily.

'Miss Haslington? I'm sorry – did I get you out of bed?' The voice was masculine and slightly mocking.

'Heavens, no.' Liri glanced at her watch. *Ten o'clock?*

'Good. I wonder if I might call some time this afternoon? I'm Colin McLeod, by the way, from Keeper's

Lodge Farm.'

Pedigree Hereford at last! Hastily Liri scrambled to her feet. Not for anything would she speak to That Man from a kneeling position.

'On business or pleasure, Mr McLeod?'

'Both, I hope. But first let me welcome you to Abbeyfield.'

Then ask in the next breath for my four acres, Liri thought acidly.

'Thank you.' She was wide awake now, her heart thudding with triumph. 'Shall we say two o'clock?'

'That will suit me fine. Goodbye for now.'

North of the border, Liri decided. Scottish name, Scottish accent.

No respecter of English rights-of-way or English orchards. A man who would almost certainly wear his clan tartan at English social functions. And he would be short and stocky, she calculated, and very conscious of his position.

But rich as he obviously was he hadn't enough money to buy her acres – because he *did* want to buy them. And it was a great pity, really, because land should be tended and nourished and worked.

If only he'd been the least bit decent, she sighed, he could have had her fields without a quibble. But there was the orchard to be avenged and the pond, and her heart took over from her head. She couldn't – *wouldn't* sell him her fields and that, until two o'clock at least, was that.

Hastily she washed and dressed, congratulating herself on having remembered to ring the dairy, then sat down to a hurried breakfast of toast and jam. But once she had finished unpacking, she promised, she really would keep regular hours and not skimp on meals just because now she lived alone. And there must be no more late mornings, she admonished, although just this once she supposed she could be forgiven for oversleeping.

Smiling she returned to her workroom and felt immediately at peace. That room at least was already comfortably familiar, and sighing deeply she drew back the curtains, allowing herself a glimpse of the spring meadows, the beech trees set bare and lacelike against a pale blue sky, the crawling tractor in a faraway field. Then abruptly she turned away. Later she would waste time in gazing, but not now. This afternoon That Man was calling and she must be ready for him, in *every* way!

Exactly at two o'clock, the door knocker echoed sharply through the house and even though she had been expecting it, Liri jumped nervously. Already she had combed her hair and renewed her lipstick.

To her annoyance she had found herself glancing in the mirror far more than was necessary and had checked the time every five minutes for the last hour.

Now Pedigree Hereford was standing on her doorstep and she hesitated for a moment, willing herself to be calm. She would be polite and distant and firm. She would not raise her voice. She would tell him that her land was not for sale, thank him for calling and that would be that. All over in five minutes. Swallowing hard she thrust out her chin then opened the door.

'Mr McLeod?' she smiled. 'Do please come in. Or would you like to sit in the garden? I've been busy unpacking and everything is still in a bit of a muddle inside, I'm afraid.'

Liri sized up her adversary. Colin McLeod was neither short nor stocky, but all of six feet. But in spite of his great advantage in height he would get as good as he gave, she asserted silently and for all his undisputed masculinity she would not allow him to intimidate her.

'The garden would be fine,' he nodded, returning her gaze. 'And I'll not mince matters, Miss Haslington. I'm here about your land, but you'll already have guessed that?'

'My land?' She gazed up at him, wide-eyed. Six feet *two* she amended. Fair hair touched with auburn; eyes indecently thick-lashed and blue. Attractive, really.

'Your fields. I'm hoping they're on the market.'

'Ah, no. I'm sorry.' Her smile was pure honey.

'But you can't farm with only four acres. A pig unit, maybe, or intensive poultry, but –'

'In a conservation area?' she demanded artlessly. 'Oh, I don't think it would be allowed.'

'Then perhaps you intend keeping a horse?'

'I don't ride.' How sweet this moment was.

'Then might I ask what you have in mind? You can't just let good land go to ruin.'

'No, I suppose not. I hadn't really given it much thought.' *Oh, Liri. Shame on you.*

'Then let me make you an offer? I can assure you we don't intend putting buildings on it – you could have that written into the agreement if you wished. But it seems wrong to let land go to waste.'

'Yes, I know,' Liri smiled. 'But you seem to have a great deal of acreage already, Mr McLeod. Surely my small fields can't make all that much difference to you?'

'Ah, but they can. Your land, though I suppose it isn't very businesslike of me to admit it, cuts a wedge into Keeper's Lodge Farm. When the herd has to be pastured on our far fields – the fields on the other side of your house, that is – they have to be herded there on the public road, and twice a day, in summer, for milking. Apart from the inconvenience, there's the risk of accidents. The herd is very valuable.'

'And my acres would remove the inconvenience and risk?'

'Exactly.' His face relaxed into a smile. Rather a nice smile, Liri thought. But one nice smile did not compensate for the closing of Pond Cottage footpath.

'I'm sorry,' she heard herself saying. 'But I have no wish at all to sell.'

'But you haven't heard what I'm willing to offer, yet.'

'It isn't a question of finance. Those fields mean more to me than money,' she said firmly.

'Miss Haslington.' The smile was gone. 'I don't think you fully appreciate the position. You'll know, of course, that an offer was made for Southgate Lodge, far in excess of your own?'

'Yes. And withdrawn,' Liri retorted primly.

'Maybe. But that offer was made by my employer and he withdrew it because he was sure you would sell him the land. He had no use for the lodge, you see, but had he anticipated your dog-in-the-manger attitude I very much doubt you would be here at all and I should not be in the invidious position of having to ask a *woman* to sell me her fields.'

'How very tiresome for you.' So Colin McLeod wasn't entirely to blame. 'And now you're going to have to tell your employer he presumed too much, I'm afraid,' Liri purred. 'None of my land is for sale or lease and now, if you'll excuse me, I have work to do.'

With a dismissive nod of her head she turned and walked away, triumph singing through her like a battle hymn.

'Miss Haslington! *Please?*'

'Good-day, Mr McLeod,' she called over her shoulder, victory smiling on her lips. Already she had made him very angry, and though he did not know it, there was worse to come. The matter of Meadowsweet Lane, for instance . . . .

She did not return to the house until she heard the slamming of the gate and the furious revving of Colin McLeod's car, but by the time she settled to the unpacking again the first flush of conquest had left her.

It wasn't Colin McLeod's fault, she conceded. Truth

known, she could have liked him if tall, blue-eyed
Scotsmen had been to her taste. She supposed that by
now he would be getting in touch with the real culprit; the
absentee owner who ran Keeper's Lodge Farm from a
desk in London or Zurich, maybe, and she wondered from
which quarter the next approach would be made.

Oh, *why* had Pedigree Hereford made her dislike him
so? She didn't need the four acres and to sell them would
almost clear her bank loan, she reasoned. But ever since
she could remember she had cared deeply for Queen's
Reach, and no faceless farmer would ever own those
beloved acres. Not ever.

It was only then that she remembered the bread and
salt.

'Drat!' she jerked, realizing they had lain unnoticed for
far too long; that early morning should have been the
time for wish-making. But it was Colin McLeod's fault,
she thought childishly. His phonecall had driven all else
from her mind.

'Oh, for goodness sake, forget it!' she chided. It was
only superstitious nonsense after all, and even if she had
remembered, her wish could never have come true. 'And
stop talking to yourself, Liri, or it'll become a habit!'

Determinedly, she scooped up the salt and placed it in
the kitchen cupboard, then throwing the rock-hard bread
into the dustbin she closed down all thoughts on the past.

Yet it would have been good to have wished, she sighed
inside her. Even if the wish had been a wasted one, it
would have been good at least to have tried.

Work! she reminded herself. Everything must be
unpacked before she went to bed tonight. And tomorrow
she would drive to York. She needed groceries and an
armchair and rugs for the living-room floor; lampshades,
too, and a sofa-bed for Connie.

*   *   *

She was standing beside the kitchen window when the man walked slowly along the lane and Liri recognized him at once.

'Tom?' she gasped, running into the garden, laughing with delight. 'Hey there! Don't dare walk past my door, Tom Cook!'

She stood at the hedge, smiling. He hadn't changed. Even the cloth cap with its brim set askew was still the same. Happy to see an old friend she opened the gate, holding out her hands in greeting.

'So it *is* you? They said at the dairy that a Miss Haslington had taken the lodge and I'll be danged if it isn't our Liri. But where did you get to, lass? You vanished without so much as a word.'

'I know Tom, and I'm sorry. It seemed the best thing to do though, at the time.'

'And where did you run away to?'

'I didn't run away. I went to college to do an art course.' Tom hadn't changed one bit. Still curious to a fault. 'I work freelance, now, designing soft furnishings and wallpaper. And I paint flower pictures, too.'

'Ah, flowers.' He seemed pleased about the flower pictures. 'Well, you'd know all about those, you being a Haslington. And you make a living from it?'

'Yes, Tom. But tell me – how is Abbeyfield?'

'Changed, Liri.' He shook his head mournfully. 'There's not many of us left since the estate got sold up. Village is full of incomers now and weekenders have bought the almshouses. And the young ones – your generation – all drifted away like you did.'

'But I've come back, Tom.'

'So you have.' He gazed pointedly at her left hand.

'Still single,' she smiled. 'A career girl, I suppose you'd call me. But my garden's a bit overgrown.' Abruptly she changed the subject. He mustn't ask about Gideon. 'I don't suppose you could straighten it out for me?'

'Glad to. No trouble at all. It's those fields of yours that've got me beat, though. Be damned if I know what made that builder do what he did. Southgate never had land to it before.'

'No, Tom.' Why was everyone fretting so about the four acres?

'Then shall you sell them, Liri?'

'I – I don't know. I haven't thought about it.'

I tell lies too, Tom. I've hardly thought about anything else.

'Well, don't do anything in a hurry. Won't be long before that builder's finished at Queen's Reach and the house'll be on the market. Whoever buys it'll be in need of a bit more land. Take my advice and think-on, Liri.'

'I will. I suppose it'll be good to have a Queen's Reach again.'

'It will, an' all. And quite a sizeable place it's going to make, by all accounts. They're knocking the stables and coach-house and Northgate Lodge into one. And the groom's old quarters, *and* the hayloft . . . .'

The hayloft. The roofspace above the loose boxes. Why did it hurt so much to remember it, still?

'I'm working on a lily and rose design.' Liri steered the conversation into safer channels. 'Do you remember Grandpa planting the rose hedge and the lilies-of-the-valley?'

'That I do. I was under-gardener, then. Those lilies'll be flowering soon – why don't you go over and take a look?'

'Will it be all right?'

'Course it will. I'm still the gardener there. Just tell the builders that Tom Cook said so,' he nodded. 'But what about *your* garden? Once I've mastered it a couple of hours a week should be enough. That suit you? Settle up every quarter-day, shall us?'

'Fine. And before you go, Tom – is Chippy Wilson still living at Woodsman's Cottage?'

'*Woodsman's?*' The gardener's head shot up. 'You haven't heard, then?'

'*Heard?*'

'Er – that Chippy's moved. He's gone to Church Cottage. Got a workshop at the back. He left Woodsman's not long after Sir Joseph died. But what might you want with Chippy?'

'Just one or two little jobs about the house,' Liri murmured. 'Shelves, and things.'

'Well, he'll be pleased to know you're back. And don't forget to help yourself to some lilies, if they're out. I reckon you're entitled.'

Smiling, Liri watched him go. Her first visitor, she thought fondly. And she need not have worried. Tom hadn't asked too many questions.

For the remainder of the afternoon Liri worked hard and just as she stood back to admire her living-room the door knocker banged loudly.

'Now who is it this time?'

Automatically she smoothed her hair and glanced quickly into the mirror. Pale still, like the *liriconfancies*. Pale-blonde hair, too, worn short in a simple cut that did things for her face. But let no one be deceived. Let no one imagine she was a pushover, she asserted silently as she hazarded a guess as to the identity of her caller.

'Sorry to disturb you again, Miss Haslington, but I won't keep you a minute,' Colin McLeod smiled.

'If it's about the land?' Liri asked abruptly.

'It is, indirectly. I've been talking to my employer. He would like to meet you tomorrow,' he smiled.

'Sorry, but I'll be shopping all day.'

Confound the man! He smiled so nicely, Liri sighed inwardly. And she shouldn't be so touchy. He was only doing his job.

'Then if Saturday isn't convenient, could you possibly make it tonight?'

'Sorry.' Tonight she was going to look at the rose hedge. 'I'm really not sure when I can fit him in. Perhaps a week Monday?'

'Not before then? But he's very anxious to —'

'Not before then,' Liri repeated. 'There's nothing to discuss anyway, and I'm really very busy.'

'Very well. I'll pass your message on, although I'm disappointed you haven't reconsidered.'

'I have not. And while you're here, I think you'd better know that I intend to have Meadowsweet Lane gated and padlocked in the very near future.' Liri flung down her trump-card. 'Perhaps you'll be good enough to tell that to your employer, too?'

'But that's ridiculous!' Colin McLeod's face reddened angrily. 'We've always used the lane!'

'Then you'll just have to accept that from now on the lane is mine and if I wish to gate it I shall do so. Exactly, I might say, as your employer has gated *his* lane.'

'I can't believe it,' Colin McLeod exploded. 'It's sheer pettiness! But what else can you expect from a — a *woman?*'

'Goodbye, Mr McLeod. And if you must call again, please try not to do it between ten and four. Those are my working hours and I don't like being disturbed.'

Immediately he had gone, Liri hurried to the window, watching his long, swinging strides, congratulating herself on the winning of round two, yet wondering at the same time exactly what she would do with her four acres.

But maybe, she pondered, they would be sold back to Queen's Reach, one day? After all, it was where they really belonged. Sighing, she dialled Connie's number.

'Well — and how's everything?' her friend demanded.

'Everything's just fine.' No need to mention Colin

McLeod. 'I've finished unpacking and I'm going out for a walk.' No need to mention Meadowsweet Lane, either. 'I feel I've earned it.'

'James rang last night,' Connie murmured. 'He phoned you yesterday afternoon, he said, but you didn't answer.'

'I was probably in the garden.' Liri's cheeks flushed pink.

There was something very unnerving about James, she thought uneasily. James could beam in on her doings with uncanny accuracy.

She supposed he would ring again tonight, just when she had returned from Queen's Reach with a heart full of memories.

'You still there, Roz? Listen, lovey, I'll hang up, now. Don't forget the flower pictures, when you have time? I'm completely sold out, now. And enjoy your walk . . . .'

If the day had been gently sunny, then the evening was sharp, a reminder that even in April, a sudden late frost was not wholly impossible.

Liri pulled on her new yellow wellingtons with childish delight, tied a silk square over her hair and shrugged into her anorak. It gave her a feeling of wellbeing to walk down Meadowsweet Lane.

Once, it had led to Queen's Reach, but now it was hers. And wild flowers would grow there again, she smiled, just as soon as That Man's cows had stopped trampling on her verges. Meadowsweet had been known as Lovers' Lane too, she recalled, but gates were easily climbed, and just as long as Pedigree Hereford got the message, couples would be welcome to come and go as they pleased.

Liri walked tall across her fields then climbed the fence at the river-path. On her right, now, was Keeper's Lodge Farm and further along, where the river looped back on itself, Woodsman's Cottage stood apart.

She turned her head away as she approached. She had no wish to look at close quarters at what had once been her home and was now the end portion of a tarted-up farmhouse. It was at this spot, Liri recalled, that she had usually met Gideon; half-way between Pond Cottage and Queen's Reach, beneath the lone copper-beech tree. It had been here he asked her to marry him; here she said yes. Yet when they decided to tell Gideon's father of their love, her happiness had shattered into a million pieces.

Gone to Canada, Grandpa told her as he gathered her into his arms and hushed her sobs.

Fiercely she slammed down her feet on the unoffending grass. Gideon was married to someone called Felicity, now. Liri had seen the announcement of their engagement in the outdated society glossy in that waiting-room and the dentist's drill had been bliss compared to the pain that stabbed mercilessly through her.

She shook her head as if to clear it of unwanted memories. The air smelled of the river and newly-turned earth and green things growing. And the walk was doing her good, assuring her that not everything in Abbeyfield had changed; that her copper-beech tree was still there. She ran her hands over its smooth, straight trunk, remembering the bread and salt and the wish that could never have come true. But she would have wished, she thought as she closed her eyes beseechingly, for just once glimpse of him. She would have asked that one day soon she would turn a corner and see him there; wished that he would look at her and say *"Liri"*, the way he used to do. She would have been content with that. Just to see him once more, hear his voice.

She opened her eyes with a gasp of derision. What superstitious nonsense! Wishing back the past, indeed! She was Rosamund Haslington, award-winning designer now, and from this moment the past was taboo!

So go home this instant, she commanded silently, and take that packet of salt and fling it to the four winds! Never mind about its being spilled. All the bad luck is behind you now. You've got your own little house and the future is wide and bright. What more do you want?

Blindly she began to run; across the field, over the paddock, past the rose hedge and the stableyard. Head down she turned into the road. Oh, damn the wish and memories of faithless lovers and damn the —

'Hey! Steady there!'

She slammed into the man and would have fallen but for hands that grasped her arms.

'Sorry!' she gasped. 'I didn't —'

She looked up, then stood shocked into rigidity. There was a sudden pain in her chest and it hurt her to breathe. Oh, please *no!*

Her heart thundered in her ears and she began to tremble, then the hands that had held her loosened their grip and she stood there swaying, almost touching him. They were too close; much, much too close.

'Liri!'

The voice was low with remembered passion; her name a caress on his lips. And the magic was back again, singing through the air, wiping away the years.

Shaking so much she could hardly stand, she forced her gaze from his, then taking a step backward because his nearness was almost unbearable she whispered, 'I'm so sorry.'

She said it in a strained, clipped voice; said it politely as though she had collided with a stranger.

Then she turned and, panic-stricken began to run. She had not dreamed it. Her arms still throbbed from the touch of his hands. He had been there, spoken her name. How could it have happened? She had only *wished.*

Somehow she inserted her key in the lock; somehow she managed to open the door. Then she slammed up the stairs and throwing herself face-down on the bed, pummelled the pillows with enraged fists.

'No!' she sobbed. 'No, no, *no!*'

But you wanted him, a voice inside her mocked. *You never forgot him. You bought this house not only because you love it but because you love him, too. You wished him back and he came, so wish him into your arms Liri. Wish him to the hayloft, where it all began . . . .*

'No!' she cried again and though the sobbing had spent itself her breathing was laboured still, her heartbeats erratic.

Swinging her feet to the floor, she reached for a tissue.

'Gideon?' she whispered. She hadn't dreamed it, so where was he now? Would he follow her, or ring her?

But her telephone was newly installed and unlisted and anyway, how could he know where she lived?

Why was he here? Surely not because she had wished for him? That was a nonsense. It had to be.

Why did you choose today to come back, Gideon? And oh, my dearest love, I'm so very, glad that you did.

She stumbled down the stairs, fixing her eyes on the phone. Of course he would ring and when he did she would not snatch up the receiver. First she would count to ten. She would count very slowly, breathing deeply and —

The phone clamoured to life so stridently and suddenly that she jumped. Snatching it up she cried, 'Hullo?'

'Roz? It's James.'

'James.' She let go her breath and sat down heavily. 'Roz? Are you there?'

'Y-yes. How are you?' He was doing it again; beaming-in when he'd no right to.

'Extremely well, and going to a party.'

'Where?' As if he could see her she dabbed again at her cheeks.

'At Verna Reid's place. Tonight's the end of the run. I

told you we only had the theatre for a month.'

'So now you'll be resting?' *Please don't let him come up to Abbeyfield.*

'Resting? Listen, my doubting darling. D'you remember Bennet Saunders? He had a serial commissioned for television.'

'Yes.'

'Well, I've landed one of the leads. *Night of the Hawkes,* a period thing. Just think of all that lovely free publicity.'

'I'm pleased for you, James.'

'Mmm. Marvellous script, in ten episodes and I'm in every one of them. Just thought I'd let you be the first to know. 'Bye, Roz. Be good.'

He put down the phone before she had time to answer and she sighed with relief. A television serial would keep him busy for months. There would be rehearsals, costume fittings, the filming, and little time left for visits to Abbeyfield.

Dully she replaced the receiver. What a mess it was. Gideon and James. Old love; new love. James who wanted her; Gideon who did not.

Why was Gideon here and why had he picked this time to visit Abbeyfield? Where was he staying and for how long? Would they meet again? And if they did, Liri winced, would *she* be with him?

Still cold inside her she knelt beside the hearth and piled logs on the fire with hands that shook

I should be miserable, she thought, but I'm not. And that should worry me, but it doesn't. All I know is that Gideon is here in Abbeyfield and maybe even thinking about me as I am thinking about him.

She tried to remember how he had seemed; if there had been pleasure in his eyes, or dismay, but she could not. After that first shattering second of recognition, she could remember nothing but his voice.

'Liri,' he had said, just as he always said it, and the old

longing had flamed inside her. And if he came to her now, would she take him in her arms, give as she had given before? Knowing all she did – would she?

This morning she would have said 'No!' but now she was not sure. Now, she would never be sure of anything again, except that she loved him still.

Four

Liri awoke with a throbbing head, remembering Gideon the instant she opened her eyes. He was here in Abbeyfield and she finally knew that in the secret deeps of her heart she had never ceased to love him. Now she was dismayed by the intensity of her feelings; afraid of meeting him again and, most cruel of all, afraid of seeing him with —

Say it, the voice of her conscience demanded. *Of seeing him with Felicity.*

And last night he had not followed her as she hoped he would; had not phoned. Tense and unhappy she lay awake, tossing and turning and thumping her pillow, and not until the small hours of the morning did she finally and fitfully sleep.

Reluctantly she drew back the curtains. The sun shone too brightly; a deceiving sun, a bringer of bad weather. Before very long there would be rain, she supposed, and all she needed was a rainy day, she sighed inwardly.

Hastily she pulled on jeans and a sweater, then pushed her feet into the bright yellow boots. She would walk away her headache and her problems, too. She would make herself remember the night she waited beside the rose hedge and the heartache that followed. She would recall the pain, the reluctant acceptance that Gideon had left her. She would remember how long it had taken to come to terms with the aloneness; the merciless way she had driven herself so there could be no time left for thoughts.

And as a result, Rosamund Haslington had gradually taken over Liri's life and the sharp edges of memory became blunted. Yet sometimes a sight, a sound or even a remembered scent had awakened the past, making it impossible to love again. After all the years, Gideon still had her heart in his keeping. She must accept that he always would.

But she would survive. She would get over the shock of last night's meeting and the pain would lessen. After all, Gideon was probably only visiting, she shrugged, and tomorrow he could well be gone again.

'I need a break,' she muttered. She was talking to herself again, but the last few days had been hectic and the shopping trip would do wonders for her deflated morale. She would take the whole day off, and when the shopping was completed, she would wander around the beautiful old city and remember good things and happy times.

Coincidence, she insisted, climbing the stile that led directly to her fields. A chance in a million, that's all it was. You won't meet him again, Liri, so stop looking over your shoulder. *Forget him.*

And she would forget the past, too. A wonderful future lay ahead; she had a home of her own and with that, she told herself firmly, she would be content.

Slowly she walked the boundaries of her fields,

listening to the sounds around her, squinting high into the sky to watch a singing, soaring lark. She had so much for which to be grateful. Gran had always insisted that a lovechild was favoured, and Gran had been right. That slight, frail-looking child had been given a very special talent and a stubborn nature, too, that refused to accept defeat.

Tilting her chin, quickening her stride, she swished through the morning-wet grass, turning her thoughts to the shopping trip. She must not forget to buy lampshades and a vase for the lilies, too. Tomorrow she would look at the rose hedge and if the lilies were in bloom —

'Oh, damn!' Lilies, lampshades, cabbages, kings – did it matter? It was useless trying not to think about Gideon, because where ever she turned now there would be something to remind her. He was as much a part of her as the air she breathed. She thought she had got over him, yet stupidly she wished him back into her life again. Turn a corner, see him walking toward you she had wished and now look where her folly had landed her!

Abruptly she turned around. She wanted to see him again and wants turned to wishes and wishes came true and she daren't, she really daren't risk meeting him again. She would return to Southgate and lay the fire and make her bed. Then she would have a shower and a mug of coffee and set out immediately for York.

Without knowing why she began to run, not stopping until Southgate's stout little door was closed behind her.

'I will forget him,' she gasped. 'I will. I *will!*'

Housework completed, Liri sighed deeply. Newly showered she pushed her feet into flat gold slippers, pulled on her favourite caftan then began to towel-dry her hair. She was feeling more relaxed, now, realizing that if all went to plan the little house would soon be ready to receive its first visitor. Connie would love it, she thought excitedly, and reaching for a pad she began to write her shopping list.

Lampshades, crusty bread, butter, cheese. And don't forget the vase for the lilies and —

She stopped, hearing footsteps outside then added *sherry* to her list. Now that Tom Cook knew of her return, perhaps she could expect visitors. She smiled, scribbled *sherry glasses*, then rose to her feet to greet the caller. Almost happy again she opened the door then stood wide-eyed with shock as Gideon Whitaker brushed past her. Hastily she slammed the door then spun round to face him, reaching for the banister rail, fighting the giddiness in her head, forcing herself to breathe evenly.

'Do come in?' Her words rasped harshly.

'For heaven's sake what's got into you, Liri? We meet again after heaven knows how long and you look at me as if you don't know me then rush off like I've got horns! This nonsense has got to stop!'

'Nonsense? I don't know what you're talking about.'

Her voice trembled, then trailed into silence.

'Of course you know! I'm talking about Meadowsweet Lane, for one thing. And while I'm about it we might as well discuss the land. I wanted those four acres. I made an offer for Southgate Lodge and Masters accepted it. Then the fool agent had to mention your name and —'

He stopped abruptly and for a moment neither of them spoke.

Liri ran her tongue round her suddenly dry lips then released her hold of the banister rail.

'You?' she gasped. 'It was *you?*'

Gideon had offered for Southgate? Then surely *he* was the faceless farmer, the Vandal who had bulldozed flat her memories? Gideon Whitaker was Pedigree Hereford.

'*You* farm Keeper's Lodge?' she gasped.

'It's mine,' he acknowledged quietly, 'although McLeod manages it. And I fully intended buying Southgate until I realized who else wanted it. I was stupid enough to think that if I withdrew my offer I could have the land I wanted and you as well.'

'*Me?*' Liri exploded. 'You – you walk out of my life without so much as a goodbye; for years I hear nothing from you, yet now you're asking me to believe you backed out for *me*? For old times' sake, was it?' The shock had lessened and now she shook with anger. 'Well, you presumed too much, Gideon Whitaker. I wouldn't sell you so much as a – a blade of grass!' She slammed to the door and flung it open. 'And now you can get out and never, ever, come near me again. We have nothing to say to each other. Not now. Not *ever!*'

Oh, why was he so good to look at, still; more handsome than ever? She closed her eyes against the need that raged suddenly and wantonly through her. Why had she been so foolish, rushing in blindly, determined to return to Abbeyfield and wallow in memories?

'Sorry, Liri, but there are things to be said.'

Gently but firmly he removed her hand from the knob and closed the door again. 'And if it's possible,' he whispered, 'you're more beautiful than ever I remembered.'

'Oh, stop it!' she hissed. 'That old cliche's been done to death. Try something more original, Gideon, like telling me where you've been all my life.'

'In Canada,' he shrugged. 'On and off.'

'And now you're managing your brother's land?'

'No. Matthew's in London, selling antiques. Keeper's Lodge Farm is mine.'

'Ha! Held up a bank, did you?'

Immediately she regretted the childish remark. Why was she letting him goad her? And why, why, *why* did she want him so?

'No,' he said quietly, his eyes unmoving on her face. 'I got lucky. My father gave me enough money to get started on in a small way and I bought some land in

Canada.'

'But of course – how stupid of me! You struck oil,' she supplied acidly, hating herself for hurting him. Because she was hurting him. She could see it in his eyes, in the tight set of his mouth.

'No, Liri. I was drilling for water as a matter of fact, and found uranium ore. The Canadian Government bought me out. Overnight I got very rich so I came back and bought what remained of Queen's Reach from Matthew. Like you, I needed to come home.'

But home to what? Liri asked herself despairingly, because even if Gideon was only an absentee owner, he would have to visit from time to time, and his comings and goings would regulate her life.

His words still beat inside her head. *I could have the land I wanted and you, as well.*

'Please go, Gideon.' Did he really think she was still available; that he had only to smile, to touch her again, and everything would be as it had been before? Was he brushing aside the heartache as if it counted for nothing?

'No, Liri. It isn't only the land. There are things to talk about, things you must know. I —'

The ringing of the phone made her start. She did not know whether to be glad, or sorry.

'Don't answer it.'

Lifting her eyes to his she saw her own torment reflected there, yet perversely she picked up the receiver.

'Yes? Who? Oh, James *darling!* How are you?' She forced her lips into a smile. 'Listen – can you ring me back? There's someone here – just leaving. No. No one of importance. Just give me a minute to get rid of him?'

Deliberately she spoke as if Gideon was in another room with a closed door between them, then blowing a kiss into the mouthpiece, she put down the receiver.

'Sorry.' She smiled brilliantly into his eyes. 'But you really *will* have to go.'

'No one of importance?' he hissed. 'My God, but you've changed. The girl I remember would never have said that.'

'Perhaps not,' she whispered. 'But you're right – people change. And they forget, too. I have.'

'Then remember *this*,' he said harshly, pulling her to him, tilting her face, searching for her mouth as she stiffened and struggled against his overpowering strength.

'No!' she gasped, but his lips found hers and his mouth was hard and demanding. At first she resisted him but he forced her lips apart with his tongue.

Her head began to swim. She was finding it hard to breathe and relaxed just long enough to take in a shuddering gasp of air.

Why were her senses playing tricks? It wasn't the hay she could smell; oh please, it couldn't be? And her heart wasn't beating madly against his and she didn't want him to hold her so tightly that she could feel his thighs hard against hers.

She felt the pressure of his hands through the flimsiness of her wrap and found herself reaching up in spite of herself, cupping his head in her hands.

His hair was still springy and thick; his need of her still darkened his eyes from grey to black. She lay limp against him, her eyes closed in exquisite submission.

Fool! screamed her reason as she lifted her lips to his again. *One last kiss?* her heart clamoured.

He released her abruptly as he had taken her, then gripping her shoulders, forced her down to the window-seat on which the telephone stood.

'That's right, Liri. Sit down and compose yourself. *James darling* will be calling back and you don't want to sound breathless, do you?'

His eyes mocked her; his mouth was taut as the jaws of a trap. Why had she let him kiss her and why had she let herself surrender to its passion? And now that he knew she still wanted him, he was looking at her with derision, lashing her with words.

Rage flamed white-hot inside her and lifting her hand she caught him a stinging slap to his cheek. Then slowly she pulled the back of her hand across her mouth as if to wipe away his kisses.

'Don't come here again,' she whispered hoarsely. 'You won't be welcome.'

She watched with dismay as he walked down the hall; sensed the anger that vibrated through him with every step he took; heard the slamming of the door.

Distraught, she began to sob; sobs born deep inside her that rose to a despairing, heart-rending cry.

'I hate you,' she cried. 'Hate you!'

Blinded by tears, she stumbled up the stairs then threw herself face-down on the bed, her body pulsating with the pain of rejection.

The phone began to ring again, but she left it unanswered. She could not speak to James; not whilst her lips throbbed from the onslaught of Gideon's kisses and need thrashed inside her still.

Covering her ears with her hands she tried to blot out the sound, yet when it eventually ceased, the ringing echoes seemed to vibrate accusingly around the house, still.

'Dear heaven,' she whispered. 'What am I to do?'

She closed her eyes, bringing his face into focus. Time had hardly touched him except to chisel his features a little more sharply. He was older, it was true, yet his dark hair was untouched by the passing of the years and still curled thickly.

She recalled his eyes, and how their greyness could change colour with his moods; eyes which had unashamedly desired her yet which only moments ago had looked at her with contempt.

But it had felt so good to be in his arms again, to feel his body against her own, to run possessive hands over the hardness of his thighs. His thighs had always excited her she admitted as the small, wanton pulses beat in unashamed time to her thoughts. They had been lean and lithe and had moved with arrogant grace. It had thrilled her just to watch him walk toward her, even, and when he had taken her in his arms —

'No!' she cried. 'Stop it! Stop it at once!'

Gideon was no longer hers. Now there was someone else in his life; maybe even children. Children, she thought dully, that another woman had given him.

So forget him, she stressed silently. Let him see he can have neither you nor your acres. Show him you are no longer available, that he can't indulge in a cheap little affair.

'And what's more,' she hissed. *'I am not leaving.'*

Not for anything would she give up Southgate, and today she would go into town as she had planned, and buy the furniture she needed. By the end of the week her little house would be a home, and when Connie visited she would tell her all, ask what was best to be done. And this time she would listen. She would do anything Connie advised – except leave Southgate, of course. She could never do that; not if it was the ruination of all she had worked for could she do that.

She reached for a tissue, blew her nose loudly and got to her feet. The storm was over. This time she had got things into their proper perspective and the very next time she came face to face with Gideon she would be totally in command of her feelings. She really would.

Much later than she had intended, Liri stopped her car outside the brick and cobble cottage that stood beside the church. She had decided to visit Chippy Wilson before she did her shopping, because now the gate had become more important than the furniture.

From a distance she heard the rhythmic swish of a woodplane and she followed the sound to the open workshop doors.

'Chippy?'

'Well now, it's Liri. Sit you down.' He nodded to a wooden trestle and laid down the plane as though he had been expecting her.

'Tom Cook told me you'd be calling; some shelves, he said?'

He picked up his pipe, clamping it between his teeth, treating her with such unconcern that eight years seemed to count for nothing at all. She could be a child again, Liri marvelled, for all the elderly carpenter seemed to have noticed.

'Good old Tom,' she laughed. 'And how are you, Chippy?'

'Fair-to-middling, thanks. Now where would you be wanting those shelves?'

'It isn't shelves,' Liri hesitated. 'What I really want is a gate. I want it exactly like the one you made for Keeper's Lodge Farm.'

'And where d'you want it?' He struck a match and ponderously held it to the tobacco in his pipe.

'At – at the top of Meadowsweet Lane.' Why did she sound so guilty?

'What ever for? Meadowsweet's never been gated – not in my time it hasn't.'

'But it must have been. There are posts —'

'Not in *my* time,' Chippy asserted.

'Well, I want it gated now. I don't mind people – it's cattle I object to.'

'And what've you got against Mister Gideon's cows, then? You and him were friends.'

'Meadowsweet Lane belongs to Southgate Lodge. I

want my privacy,' Liri countered.

'Won't be very private when he buys your land, Liri Haslington.'

'Who says he's buying my land?'

'Well isn't he?'

'No, he's not,' she grated, 'and that's a fact. My land isn't for sale.'

Cussed and stubborn, Chippy was; always had been, Liri fumed. And far too direct for comfort. Talking to her as if she were still a child; asking questions in the same blunt manner. Treating her as if –

As if she were one of themselves, her sub-conscious supplied. As if she hadn't changed. One of their own, still, and not a successful designer. A compliment, really.

'Anyway, why did you go off like you did, lass, saying nothing to nobody?'

'The *gate*, Chippy.'

Dear, unchanging Abbeyfield. Any day now, they'd hear that Mafeking had been relieved.

'Don't know as how I can manage it, Liri. Can't take sides.'

'Sides? You talk as if there's trouble.'

'And isn't there? Would you be gating Meadowsweet Lane if you weren't set on trouble?'

'*He* did it!' she flared. 'What about Pond Cottage footpath, then?' She was becoming annoyed and worse than that, she sounded petty and childish. She breathed in deeply and tried again.

'Sorry. I shouldn't have spoken like that. But I *would* like a gate, please.'

She had said it almost beseechingly, drat it. Whose lane was it, anyway?

'None of this would've happened,' came the grumbling reply, 'if Mister Gideon had bought Southgate when it came on to the market. But I suppose Woodsman's is bigger —'

'Woodsman's? He *lives* there?' Dismay hit Liri like a slap. 'Permanently, you mean?'

'You didn't know? Tom didn't tell you?'

'No, he didn't.'

Pedigree Hereford. A faceless farmer in London or Zurich, she had thought. Yet Gideon lived so near she could see the smoke from his chimney, and at night the glow from his upstairs window.

'No accounting for taste, I suppose. My missus was glad to leave there. Too lonely for her. But it seems to suit young Gideon.' He shrugged and laid down his pipe. 'Ah, well. Sorry about the gate, Liri.'

'You mean you won't make it for me? Then you *are* taking sides. You're siding with *him!*'

'I'm sitting on the fence. I want no part of it. I don't rightly know what's happening but I can't see any need for that gate, except spite. I don't understand you, Liri lass. You're acting peevish. I thought at one time your gran had made a good job of rearing you, but it seems I was wrong.'

He picked up his plane and began swinging it along the wood edge again, his mouth a downcurve of disapproval.

'Chippy?' Liri gasped, but he ignored her completely, and it was like a reprimand; as if he had slapped her, almost. And it hurt. It hurt a lot.

She turned abruptly. 'Bye,' she whispered, but he made no reply.

How could he? Liri fumed. A gate, that was all she had asked for, she thought incredulously as she slammed shut the door of her car. A simple, white-painted gate at the top of Meadowsweet Lane; *her* lane.

But Chippy had been adamant. Spiteful, he'd called her. What had she got against Gideon? he had demanded.

Interfering, that's what he was. Acting as if he had a right to know every last iota of her business; giving advice she did not want and had no intention of taking. And if he wouldn't make that gate, she choked inside her, then she would find someone who would!

Yet was Chippy really to blame? Liri willed herself to be calm. Wasn't it *her* fault – hers and Gideon's – and the past catching up with the present? And now there was something else to make life even more unpleasant. Gideon was living in Abbeyfield and life would be utterly unbearable.

Sooner or later they would meet again – village life would demand it – and then the humiliation would begin.

'Petrol,' she whispered dully, remembering that the last time she had driven the car the gauge had been almost at empty.

That's right, Liri. Close your thoughts down again. Stick your head in the sand; the mess will still be waiting when you decide to surface.

She looked down then let go an exclamation of annoyance. Her handbag. She had left it on Chippy's workshop bench.

With mixed feelings she opened the car door, but at least now she had an excuse to go back and apologize.

'You left your purse,' Chippy said when he saw her standing there again.

'Yes. And I'm sorry. I – I shouldn't have slammed off like that.'

'Nothing to be sorry about, Liri. But something's wrong between you and Gideon and it's got me beat. Can't the two of you take up where you left off? Folks around these parts al'us thought you were close, once. Why don't you sort our your differences like two reasonable people?'

'No, Chippy.' He just didn't know how deep the wound had gone. 'I want Meadowsweet Lane closed – that's all there is to talk about as far as I'm concerned.'

It was nothing to do with village opinion. Gideon had put up a gate, why then couldn't she?

For just a moment she allowed herself to think of the

additional inconvenience she would be heaping upon
Colin McLeod. With the coming of the warmer weather
the herd would spend both day and night in the fields and
twice a day they would have to be walked along the road
for milking. And the closing of Meadowsweet Lane would
make their cumbersome journey even longer, she thought
with brief regret. But Gideon had presumed too much,
she reminded herself defiantly. First her land and now
her lane. Well, he wasn't getting either.

'*Closed,* Chippy,' she asserted.

'All right. If you want to be awkward, then it's entirely
up to you,' the old man muttered. 'But what about all the
courting that goes on down there? The young ones aren't
going to be pleased.'

'Gates can be climbed, Chippy. It isn't people I object to,
it's those Herefords.'

'Gideon's Herefords.'

'All right. *Gideon's* Herefords,' Liri hissed. 'I don't care
who they belong to, they're not using my lane and that's
my last word!'

Shaking with dismay she turned abruptly and walked
away. Trouble was, she reflected, that Chippy Wilson was
right; so why couldn't she take his advice?

'Bye,' she called over her shoulder.

'Pah! Awkward, that's what you are! Growed up into a
woman, that's what you've done,' he called after her. 'But
I'm not making that gate, Missy. Be danged if I will!'

Deflated and bewildered, Liri drove away, glancing in
the mirror to see him standing at his gate, his mouth
pursed tight with disapproval.

What a mess it was, she thought despairingly, and this
should have been such a marvellous day. Now everything
was going wrong. She had upset Chippy who sided openly
with Gideon. And Gideon not only lived in Abbeyfield,
but lived less than half a mile away.

But why in Woodsman's Cottage? Why not the larger,

more modern farmhouse? Surely Woodsman's could only be a *pied-a-terre*, a country cottage to be used when he visited the farm? Surely the aristocratic Felicity would not live in such a small, old-fashioned house?

But maybe she would? She could, perhaps, be the kind of person who would be perfectly happy to do just that. She might even be a very nice person and one, Liri frowned, who would prove extremely hard to dislike.

A garage loomed ahead and she dropped a gear and glanced in the mirror.

Petrol, she reminded herself. And then on to the furniture shops, so that Connie could visit.

I've got myself into a real mess, she thought sadly, and the sooner I can tell Connie about it, the better.

If only Gideon had not been here. If only he had not kissed her, she sighed.

But he *was* here, and he *had* kissed her; a kiss she could not forget. A kiss, if she were completely honest, she did not want to forget.

And that was where it all became so very complicated, because kissing a married man was one thing – enjoying it was altogether another. Skating on thin ice it was called, and if she didn't take care she would be up to her stubborn chin in muddy water. Very muddy water indeed.

Five

Liri checked the station clock yet again. Waiting for trains, she conceded, had always thrilled her. The overwhelming noise; the sudden hustle and bustle and banging-open of doors; of friends greeting and lovers meeting.

Connie is coming, she whispered happily inside her, and my home is ready to welcome her.

She recalled the pride with which she made a final check before leaving for the station. The new furniture had arrived and immediately the little house had come to life she had thought, sniffing contentedly at the mingling scents of polish and narcissi. Appraisingly her eyes had swept the room. The stone hearth was scrubbed clean and in the iron grate the fire lay ready to be lit. On the floor beside it stood a basket of logs; on the wall the brass toasting-fork gleamed. On either side of the hearth stood a moss-green sofa-bed and matching armchair and between them a long, low coffee table.

Liri gazed critically at the drape of the curtains and the plump, matching cushions. The design still gave her satisfaction, for it had earned the coveted award and her first taste of success. She had named it *Woodlands,* a tangle of leaves in every imaginable shade of green, with white-spotted russet toadstools in sharp contrast. Those toadstools had grown in the beechwood and found their way to her easel from the dim mists of memory. And now, although she still looked on herself as a freelance, she worked almost exclusively for Hathaway-Paige, the manufacturers who had taken up *Woodlands* and made it into a classic, almost.

Still smiling contentment she stepped into the small, square hall, glancing into the gilt-framed mirror that hung above the half-console table, then up the newly-carpeted stairs to the half-landing where a vase frothed over with cherry blossom.

Almost reluctantly she had closed the door on it all, then set out to meet Connie's train and now as she waited, she felt a fresh surge of excitement as the blue and yellow engine swayed round the curving track and into the station.

Liri glanced to either side. She had taken up a position in the centre of the platform although she knew it would have been far better to have waited beside the barrier. Would Connie be at the front of the train? Liri frowned as doors began to open and people getting off became entangled with people getting on. Most likely in one of the centre carriages, she decided. Connie was a centre person who did everything in moderation and saw both sides with equal clarity.

Then hands gripped Liri's shoulders and she spun round to greet her friend.

'Con!'

'Hi. Let's have a look at you,' came the nonchalant reply.

'Have I grown?' Liri laughed. 'It's been all of ten days, you know.'

'You don't look so bad, considering —'

'Considering what?'

Liri picked up the small case, shepherding her friend toward the barrier, but she did not get a reply. She shouldn't have expected one, come to think of it. Connie had always doubted the wisdom of the move north, so now she must be convinced it had been a good one.

'Look at our walls,' Liri smiled proudly as they left the station precinct and headed for the car-park. 'Old as time, those walls, and still perfect. The second city in England, this used to be.'

'Only the *second?*' Connie teased, settling herself in the passenger seat, painstakingly fastening her seat-belt.

'Next time you come we'll spend a day here,' Liri smiled, 'but right now there's so much talking to do. You'll like the house, Con. I've just about got myself straightened out.'

'Good, because I've an order for a set of flower pictures. I hope the move hasn't upset your rhythm!'

'Quite the opposite.' Liri frowned at the traffic lights ahead, willing them to stay on green. 'I have something to work for, now. I've got Southgate. I've come home.'

'OK.' Connie held up her hands in mock surrender. 'I'm convinced. My, but you're a clannish lot, you northerners. You're worse than the Scots.'

'Ooh, yes. And talking about Scots – I've discovered who Pedigree Hereford is.' They had left the narrow old streets behind them now and Liri was able to relax a little. 'I – I didn't tell you when you rang because – well, it came to blows between us, as a matter of fact.'

The words came out in a torrent and not the carefully regulated trickle Liri had rehearsed. But best get it over with. Connie would find out, anyway. She always did.

'Blows?' Connie's eyebrows swerved upward. 'And

what's the name of this spoiler, then; this tearer-out of all things sacred?'

Liri gazed ahead with studied unconcern then ran her tongue around her lips.

'Look – we're out in the country now; the farmland, Con. Did you ever see anything so beautiful, so – so bounteous?'

'What's he called, Roz?'

'Er – Colin McLeod.' No use trying to outwit Connie. 'Or so I first thought.'

'But?'

'But he's only the farm manager and – oh, will you look at the outline of that beech tree, Con? And soon it'll be covered with lovely pale green leaves. I can see the most beautiful beech wood from my bedroom window –'

'Pedigree Hereford?' Connie prompted, her voice low and demanding to be answered.

'All right.' Liri's chin jutted stubbornly. 'If you must know it's – it's Gideon Whitaker.'

'Holy Cow! I might have known it! Come to think of it, I think I always did. Why didn't I tie you to the table-leg like my instincts told me?'

'Hold on. There's more to come.' Liri took a deep breath, determined now she had started to hold nothing back. 'He's – he's living in Abbeyfield, too. He's so near, in fact, that I can see his cottage from my studio window. And before you blow your top, I *swear* I didn't know. I honestly thought he was in Canada.'

'And this brush you had with him? What was it about?' The eyes that met Liri's in the driving-mirror demanded the whole truth.

'Well, it started with Colin McLeod asking me to sell him the four acres. Naturally I said I wouldn't,' Liri shrugged. 'Then – then I told him I intended closing Meadowsweet Lane, as well.'

'Clever girl.' Connie's face contorted into an expression

of martyrdom. 'You don't do things by halves, do you?'

'He didn't like it a bit,' Liri rushed on. 'He told me that his employer had made an offer for Southgate Lodge and withdrawn — '

'Say no more.' Connie's eyes swept beseechingly heavenward. 'His employer – Gideon Whitaker, no less – thought you'd be putty in his hands?'

'Exactly. Gideon came to see me and – and that's when I slapped him.'

'Oh my Lord! I let you out of my sight for ten days and you're up to your stubborn little neck in trouble.' She stopped, shaking her head, sighing eloquently.

'I'm *not* in trouble, Con – well, nothing I can't handle.' Liri lifted her foot from the accelerator, swerving to avoid a cock-pheasant that darted across the road ahead of them.

'Watch what you're doing!' Connie let go her indrawn breath as the large, bright bird disappeared into the hedgerow. 'OK. So I believe you when you say you didn't know lover-boy was around, but if you had known would it have made any difference, Roz? Would you have come here if you'd known he was living so near?'

'Yes. I think at the time I would.' Liri faltered. 'I'm almost sure I was still in love with him – or with the memory of being in love with him. But then he came to see me and acted just like nothing had happened; like he hadn't walked out on me, or anything.' No need to go into detail about those kisses or the havoc they unleashed. 'So I gave him his marching orders.' No need, either, to mention the exquisite pain that iced through her when she learned that Gideon lived at Woodsman's Cottage.

'And his wife?' Connie pressed.

'I haven't met her yet but I shall, I suppose. There'll be no way of avoiding it in a place as small as Abbeyfield. I keep hoping she'll be a snooty cat so I don't have to like her.'

'You realize none of this would have happened if you'd stayed in London?' Connie gave an exasperated snort. 'But it isn't too late. You could get out without losing too much money. I always thought that coming up here was a bit mad, anyway.'

'Sorry, but I'm not selling out. At least I know now where I stand with Gideon. And if I came back to London there'd be James to contend with.'

'Oh, Roz. You really go the whole hog, don't you?'

'I suppose I do,' she murmured, relieved the worst was over. 'And by the way – people call me Liri, here. Just thought I'd remind you. Oh, take a look at that view? It stretches into forever, doesn't it?'

'Very lovely, but don't try to change the subject. We were about to discuss James Howard.'

'No we weren't, because there's nothing to discuss. I can't marry him. I've always known it, really. I think he only wants me because he can't have me. One night of passion, and he'd be on his way.'

'Gideon Whitaker's at the bottom of all this,' Connie growled. 'If you can't have him you're not having anyone? Is that it?'

'I don't want him,' Liri pouted. 'And didn't you once say something about half a loaf – about even giving up bread altogether? If you're happy being a career girl, why can't I be?'

'You've got me there. And it's none of my business, really. But I worry about you. I don't know how deeply you felt for Gideon Whitaker but I know you well enough to realize the wound went deep.' Connie's eyes were bright with concern. 'I don't want you to be hurt again, that's all.'

'Don't worry. I'm not going to do anything stupid as far as Gideon's concerned,' Liri choked, tight-lipped. 'I couldn't, anyway. They're still a bit old-fashioned about things like that in Abbeyfield. The village would be down on us like a ton of bricks if we started an affair. But I can't – *won't* – marry James. I'm sure of it now and as soon as I can I'll come down to London and tell him so.'

Then the subject of lovers past and lovers present came to an abrupt halt as they reached Abbeyfield.

'Welcome to Southgate,' Liri whispered, turning into Meadowsweet Lane. 'W– what do you think, Con?'

'Not bad. Not bad at all.' Connie was smiling, in fact, when the room-to-room inspection was over. 'OK, Roz. You win. I've got to admit you've got yourself a darling of a place – and a good investment, too,' she added hastily.

'Shall I show you the fields, or would you like to have a stroll on your own while I get the meal on the table?' Liri smiled tremulously

'Think I'd like to stretch my legs and breathe some country air if you don't mind. Just point me in the direction of those hallowed acres and I'll make up my own mind if they're worth all the trouble they're causing,' she grimaced.

'It rained this morning so you'd better put my wellingtons on. And they're not hallowed acres, Con. I think of them as the *beloved* acres. Cross the stile at the end of the lane and the two fields on either side of you are mine. Beyond them you'll be on Keeper's Lodge land, so take care. The bull is the one with the short fat legs and a ring through his nose,' she teased.

She watched her friend go then hugged herself ecstatically. This was a happy day; a golden day to be recalled from memory and lived again if ever things went wrong.

But nothing more would go wrong, Liri insisted silently. She wouldn't let it. She had her work and her little house and Connie was the best friend anyone could want. There were complications of course, but she had finally made up her mind about James and about Gideon, too. James she would be honest with; tell him firmly there was no future for them together. And Gideon – she closed her eyes despairingly. There was no evading the fact that Gideon was another matter entirely and could not be so easily dismissed. He still had the power to disturb her.

To disturb your *pride*, she corrected silently.

But she would forget him. Soon now she would find he didn't matter as much as she had thought.

'Give it time, Liri,' she whispered fiercely. 'Only give it time . . . .'

'Clever girl,' she smiled as Connie walked into the kitchen, sniffing appreciatively. 'You timed it nicely. Supper's just ready.'

'Smells marvellous. Nothing like country air.' Connie kicked off the borrowed boots. 'Think I'll have to buy myself some wellies if I'm going to be coming here regularly. There's something rather nice about walking through wet grass.'

'Oh, Con. You haven't been through a hayfield, or anything?'

Liri closed her eyes, conjuring up a picture of her friend, happily swishing her way through a field of standing hay, or, far worse, through young green wheat.

'No. I kept to the headlands. No damage done.'

'Headlands?' Liri frowned.

'That's right. The narrow, uncultivated strip on the edge of a field. The bit the tractor can't get at, to plough.'

'I know. I was just wondering where you'd picked up the information, that's all.'

'From the handsome Scot – who else?' Connie grinned. 'He went to great lengths to explain where townies should walk, as a matter of fact. He's rather a dish, wouldn't you say?'

'If you like haggis,' Liri retorted. 'But right now I'd prefer chicken in mushroom sauce – and like I said, it's ready.'

Liri frowned. So Colin McLeod was interfering again?

'Where did you meet him?' she demanded, lifting the casserole to the table.

'Looking over the hedge, actually; gazing intently at your bottom field. He says he'll cut your hay if you'd like him to and I told him it sounded a good idea. Seems the builder fellow you bought this house from had some arrangement with Keeper's Lodge Farm about the hay crop — '

'Keeper's Lodge Farm has all the hay it wants,' Liri retorted tartly. 'They can keep their grasping hands off *mine.*'

'But that's not entirely fair, is it? Hay isn't just tall grass, you know. It needs cultivating and dressing and Keeper's Lodge Farm always did that for the builder and — '

'And they think they're going to do the same for me? Well, they're not, Con.'

'So you'll let those fields grow rough, will you, rather than —'

'My, but the silent Scot has really been putting it over,' Liri hissed. 'All you need to know about country matters in one easy lesson. Don't you see he's trying to get at me through you, now?'

'No, I don't,' Connie defended. 'I found him very interesting to talk to. What he said made sense.'

'It makes sense to me too, but I'll advertise the hay crop in the local paper when the time comes. Some farmer's sure to want it.' Liri spooned potatoes on to her plate. 'If they'll cut it, they can have it.'

'And if no one wants it you'll be left with egg on your face, won't you? Besides, Colin McLeod has already put a spring dressing on your fields so you should give him first refusal.'

'On *Mr Master's fields,*' Liri corrected. 'They were

nothing to do with me, then.'

'OK. Sorry I spoke,' Connie grinned maddeningly. 'Let's forget it.'

'Let's. I don't want to talk about Mr McLeod, charming though you seem to find him. Unless you found out anything – er – anything else, that is? Like – like a bit of local gossip? I'm still out of touch. I've hardly set foot in the village since I came,' Liri explained hastily.

'No gossip. We talked mostly about crops and headlands and your hay. And about Flora.'

'So he *is* interested in the opposite sex?' Liri retorted gleefully.

'Idiot. Flora's a young cow,' came the smug reply. 'Seems he reared her from a calf. He reckons she's just about perfect and her first calf is going to be perfect, too. It's due any day, I believe. He's like an expectant father.'

'You're quite incorrigible,' Liri gasped. 'I think you've made a conquest.'

'Ha!'

'No, truly. And I think you're being evasive. You've got that look in your eyes, Connie Davies. There's something else, isn't there?'

'I'm hungry.' Connie took up her knife and fork. 'And this chicken smells good. So do you mind if we eat first and finish the inquisition later?'

'You *do* know something!'

'Later, I said. And if you don't want that last potato?'

They ate in near-silence and finally Connie pushed aside her plate.

'I enjoyed that. You'll make some man a good wife, one day. Ever thought about taking the plunge, Roz?'

'Don't spoil things? You know the way things are, Con. Let's keep James out of it, shall we?'

'It wasn't James I had in mind.' Connie pushed back her chair. 'I'll clear the table if you'll make the coffee. We'll take it into the sitting-room and have it by the fire, uh? I've bought you a present, by the way – well, for the house, actually. I'll just pop upstairs and get it from my case.'

Liri smiled contentedly. She adored presents and never said, *Oh, but you shouldn't have.* Not even to James. And she wasn't marrying James, she reminded herself. Come to think of it, it seemed she wouldn't be marrying anybody. A dedicated career girl? No bread? Just Abbeyfield and growing old gracefully, with a running feud with Keeper's Lodge Farm as her only preoccupation?

My acres, she thought. Gideon shall *not* have them. Not even the hay.

'Here you are!' Connie carried a parcel in one hand and a bottle of brandy in the other. 'Let's drink to success!' Excitedly Liri opened the package then gasped, 'They're beautiful!' Two crystal brandy glasses lay side by side in a velvet-covered box. 'Oh, thank you!'

'Thought I'd start off your collection.' Connie was obviously pleased. 'Tell you what – let's pretend we're back at the flat. Let's leave the washing-up and natter, instead?'

'Let's,' Liri laughed, suddenly so happy that all the disturbing events of the past ten days faded as the April evening was fading. 'Shall I close the curtains?'

Connie shook her head. 'Just sit down and relax. Small coffees and large brandies, uh?'

Liri gazed reflectively into her friend's face. She *was* keeping something back. Her expression positively oozed smugness.

'Tell me the news, Con? Is it something to do with my flower pictures?'

'Nope.'

'All right, then. The Flying Scotsman's asked you for a date?'

'Ha. Who's being funny?'

'Well, there *is* something,' Liri frowned. 'I know you too well to —'

'OK. Suppose you've got to know.' With deliberate concentration Connie laid the tray on the long, low table. 'And don't pick up that coffee-pot. It's rather a nice one and I wouldn't want you to drop it. I'll pour, if you don't mind.'

Bemused, Liri waited.

'Sit down,' she was ordered, 'because I'm going to tell you something that's going to knock you sideways. Now which way do you want it? Nice and easy, or straight from the shoulder?'

'Con?' Strange things were happening in the pit of Liri's stomach, like it was full of butterflies wearing seaboots. 'Please?'

'One glug, or six?' Connie poured brandy into the glasses.

'*For goodness sake!*' Liri gasped.

'Cheers.' Connie held up her glass. 'And Gideon Whitaker isn't married, by the way.'

'*Wha-a-at!*' The butterflies were suddenly still and ice-cold shock stiffened Liri's body. 'Con – say you're not joking? Say it again – slowly?'

'No fooling. He's single. Colin McLeod told me,' came the quiet reply. 'I asked him if he was sure and he said sure he was sure. And for goodness sake drink that brandy. You look as if you need it.'

'B-but his engagement announcement. I saw it. *I did.*'

Liri reached for the glass and lifted it to her lips. Oh dear lovely heaven, he wasn't married. *He – wasn't – married!*

'Well, whatever you thought, it seems you got it wrong. As far as I could make out there have been a few dalliances and once a doting mama thought she'd got him cornered. But the fact remains, it seems, that the said Mr Whitaker is up for grabs. So what's keeping you?'

'I – I don't know, Con.' None of this was happening. It *couldn't* be. 'Suddenly you fling it at me. You tell me what should be the most wonderful news —'

'*Should* be?'

'Well, what about his engagement? I saw that announcement,' Liri choked. 'I really did.' She couldn't believe he was free. She dare not.

'Engagements get broken, Roz.'

'But he left me. One minute we were going to tell Sir Joseph about us and the next –'

'All right. So I'll admit it needs a bit of sorting out, but why not give him a chance? Try something like, "By the way, Gideon – that date we had all those years ago, et cetera, et cetera". He'll probably have a perfectly valid explanation.'

'I don't doubt that,' Liri whispered. 'But if he'd cared all that much, wouldn't he have tried to find me?'

'How do you know he didn't? Weren't you determined not to be found? You sold up, handed in the key and vanished, you told me.'

'I suppose I did. And I'm not trying to play devil's advocate, truly I'm not. It's only that – well, it takes a bit of getting used to.' She emptied her glass at a gulp, then sucking in her breath she gasped, 'Ouch.'

'Hey! That stuff's supposed to be warmed and sniffed and sipped.'

'I know.' Liri held out her glass for more. 'But the circumstances are rather – well, you did say you were going to knock me sideways.'

She was shaking, now. She felt sick and happy and glad and afraid. And at the drop of Tom Cook's cap, she thought hysterically, she would burst into big, beautiful tears.

'Sideways? I did and I have, it seems. You're white as a sheet. But what are you going to do about it?'

'I don't know, Con. Right now, I honestly don't know.'

She closed her eyes and took a slow, shuddering breath. 'I'm afraid. Supposing he isn't interested any longer?'

'I don't imagine he got his face slapped for being indifferent,' came the flat retort. 'I think you should see him – but tomorrow, when you've come down to earth, I mean. Sleep on it.'

'Y-yes. That's it.' Sleep? Oh dear, sweet heaven . . . .

For the rest of the evening they talked spasmodically, but Liri had little recollection of what was said. Mostly she gazed into the wood-flames, trying to conjure up Gideon's face but maddeningly it refused to materialize and all she could hear was his voice.

'. . . I realized I could have the land I wanted, and you as well.'

Why hadn't he told her then he wasn't married? If he'd wanted her as much as she wanted him, he'd have said it. But eight years is a long time, she sighed inside her. He could have changed.

Yet the phonecall from James had annoyed him, she mused, smiling. 'Then remember this . . . .'

Yes, she still remembered that kiss; the feel of his hands with only the flimsiness of her wrap between them and her eager, naked body. She loved him more than ever, if that were possible, but now she was afraid. Had the years between divided them? Had her coldness finally killed in him what feelings might have remained?

'I'm tired,' Connie yawned, 'and since you're smiling enigmatically down from your pretty pink cloud and haven't heard one word I've said for the last hour, don't you think we might call it a day? I take it I'm sleeping in the studio?'

Liri stretched and half-opened her eyes. 'You are. And y'know what, Connie Davies? You're the best friend a girl ever had. Did I ever tell you?' Any minute now she would weep. She *would*.

'No, you didn't. But you're absolutely right, of course.' She smiled and kissed Liri affectionately. 'And I know it sounds crazy, but try to get some sleep.'

'I will,' Liri whispered. 'Oh, I *will*.'

To sleep and hopefully to dream. To dream of Gideon and his hard, demanding kisses; to awaken to a morning bright with promise; to turn a corner and see him there, walking toward her, exactly as she had wished.

I laid my hands on the beech tree, she marvelled as she lay wide-eyed in the silent darkness, and I wished for him. And soon I shall see him, and when I do, what will I say?

Would she tell him she loved him; say it outright as easily as she had been able to say it in the days before —

She threw back the quilt with an exasperated cluck then drew aside the curtains to gaze out into the night.

A lamp burned in the upstairs window at Woodsman's Cottage. Gideon was at home and reading, most likely. Did he have a bedside phone and dare she ring him? Not to speak to him, of course; just to hear his 'Hullo?'

But she didn't know his number although it should be there, in the phone-book. And why, she thought impatiently, hadn't she thought of it before? Why hadn't she opened the directory, trailed her finger down the Ws, and seen his name and address there? Why had Connie found out in minutes what she herself had failed to discover in eight unhappy years? And why was she standing here now, so terribly afraid?

So many whys, Liri shivered, creeping back to bed to lay wide-eyed again, peering through the half light at the uncaring ceiling.

Gideon? She sent her thoughts winging. *I love you so much, but something is making me afraid. Help me? Please help me, my darling.*

*   *   *

By unspoken agreement, Gideon's name was not mentioned for the remainder of the weekend, because once having dropped her bombshell Connie Davies seemed smugly content to sit back and allow the dust to settle.

From Liri's point of view, however, it was a completely different matter. Hardly for a moment was Gideon absent from her thoughts and she swung erratically from high to low; from joy to doubt.

Gideon was not married and living here, in Abbeyfield. And they would meet soon, and he would say —

What *would* he say? She had been cold. She had even slapped him. But he had kissed her, she thought, relaxing into daydreams again. And he had shown anger, jealousy even, when James phoned.

Gideon had held her intimately and the feel of his hands, the touch of his lips, had been urgent and demanding and exactly as it had always been. Yet when they met, she frowned, he had said nothing. He should have asked her.

'Liri darling,' he should have said, 'where did you go? I looked for you . . . .'

But had he looked for her, and for how long? When did Felicity enter his life, and why had they not married?

In the end it was Connie who, in her usual uncompromising manner, had placed the whole bewildering matter into a small, neat nutshell.

'So see you next Friday night, Roz?' They were waiting for the London train. 'And could you possibly have dragged yourself back down to earth by then? Might I even expect a picture or two?'

'Sorry, Con. Has it been awful for you, this weekend?'

'Not a bit. I've enjoyed myself a lot. But get the Gideon affair sorted.'

'I don't quite know how,' Liri faltered. 'I think I should let it happen naturally, sort of.'

'I entirely agree. Naturally – like heaving a brick through his window. Then having attracted his attention you might casually enquire where he's been, these past few years. Do it quietly, of course, and with dignity – with your foot firmly on his throat.'

'You're an idiot,' Liri laughed.

'I know. It's one of my many endearing qualities. But seriously, though, I think you should bring things into the open. If you really want to, that is.'

'I want to,' Liri whispered. 'I've always wanted to. There's never been anyone else.'

'I'd rather gathered that,' came the bland retort. 'But remember there's the James affair to be straightened out as well. And before very much longer, if what my instincts tell me is true.'

'He isn't going to like it,' Liri sighed.

'You're right. He won't. He'll protest very dramatically, I shouldn't wonder. But James makes a production of everything and he'll get over it. After all, you weren't lovers, exactly.'

'We weren't lovers, *period*,' Liri shrugged. 'There was only ever Gideon.'

'OK. So see Gideon —' Connie held her counsel until the station announcer had confirmed the approach of the London train. 'You know you're longing to. Then get down to work again, uh?'

'I will. And 'bye, Con. It's been lovely having you,' she smiled.

'I've enjoyed it a lot. I'll phone later in the week and let you know which train I'll be getting.'

'Yes. Do that. And buy yourself those wellingtons.' '

'I will. And some woolly socks.'

Inconsequential chatter to fill the departing moments as doors slammed and windows were slid down.

'Look after yourself.'

'And you.'

Liri was standing there long after the train had gone, thinking how perfect her world had become; thinking about her work; her lovely home. Thinking about Abbeyfield and dear, dear Connie and how Gideon wasn't married, after all. And she was so happy she wanted to burst into tears of pure joy. Lovely, lovely tears. Right there in the middle of platform 14.

Six

Liri drove slowly back to Abbeyfield, loving the spring evening, the unfurling leaves, the trees heavy with blossom.

'Gideon Whitaker.' Softly she breathed his name. Second son of Sir Joseph, 10th baronet, she smiled gently. Thirty-two in June. Tall, dark, grey-eyed, with muscular arms and the broad shoulders of a man who farms the land. Gideon her first love; her only love. Gideon who left her and who soon would tell her why.

Reluctantly she turned off her thoughts, pulling the car over to the grass verge, switching off the ignition as a herd of cows lurched back to the pasture after afternoon milking.

She wound down the window and watched their slow passing, listening to the heavy measured breathing; marvelling that such large, clumsy animals could walk with so little sound.

She counted sixty-two in all, then smiled at the

herdsman who nodded his thanks. She wanted to smile at everyone. Her world was suddenly so full of wonder that she was afraid it might stop spinning.

'. . . *and Gideon Whitaker isn't married, by the way.*'

Words of magic, dropped with such nonchalance. Words which even yet made her heart beat faster. She was still a little disbelieving about everything. It was like the year, she recalled, when she had set her heart on a bicycle for Christmas.

'Will it cost too much, Gran?'

'We'll see,' came the non-committal reply.

'Second-hand would be fine,' she had confided anxiously to Grandpa and he'd looked at Gran and they'd nodded to each other. 'We'll see . . . .'

She had known the bicycle would be there on Christmas morning, but weeks of nagging doubt had somehow added to the magic. And it was the same now, with Gideon. She knew she loved him and was almost sure he still loved her. She had seen it in his eyes, even as she raised her hand to strike him.

There would be an explanation. They would be lovers again and this time they would be married.

She took a deep, tremulous breath. Everything in her world seemed so perfect she wondered why she had stayed away from Abbeyfield for so long.

'It *will* be all right,' she whispered, as she turned into Meadowsweet Lane. 'Soon now I shall meet him . . . .'

With Connie gone the little house seemed strangely silent, Liri thought as she looked out across her fields to Woodsman's Cottage. It was too early yet for lights and there was no smoke from either chimney. But maybe Gideon was at Keeper's Lodge Farm, or away for the weekend? Perhaps he'd gone to Canada again?

'Stop it! ' she urged. 'Let things happen and *don't*

worry.'

But for all her resolve she found herself pulling on wellingtons and anorak. She would walk over her fields instead, look at the growing grass, make a decision about the hay crop. And while she was looking, she would think things out; whether or not she should phone Gideon; whether she should walk over to Woodsman's; what she should say.

She closed her eyes and sighed blissfully. *Gideon is not married.* One day she would embroider those wonderful words on canvas and have them framed.

She laughed nervously, dug her hands deep into her pockets and made for the stile at the end of the lane.

The dew-damp grass squeaked beneath the soles of her boots and she took deep, steadying breaths of the cool, scented air. Already the sky was darkening and the cawing of the rooks in the oak tree was no more now than an occasional sleepy k-a-ark. In the pine tree a lone thrush sang a last evening song.

My world is so beautiful, she thought. I am so lucky that any time now things will begin to go wrong again.

She forced herself to think about the Christmas bicycle. It had been there. Second-hand, but painted a bright spanking red, with a shiny new bell and a little cane basket at the front. She needn't have worried. She shouldn't be worrying now.

Deliberately she considered her fields. The grass was growing as everything grew in April, and tomorrow she would awaken to May Day and the loveliest of all the months.

She leaned on the gate, chin on hand, and gazed absently over Peterkin Paddock. It wasn't a paddock now of course and the ponies that once grazed there were gone. It had been such a beautiful little field, Liri considered, its hedges thick and most times uncut, with so many wild flowers growing there; celandines, dog violets and foxgloves, and honeysuckle, climbing up through the hawthorn. And brambles in the autumn, she recalled; black and fat and juicy.

She realized she must have been gazing at Gideon for several seconds before he became a part of her daydreaming. He floated mistily into the picture from the past then stood clearly in focus beside the gate at the far end of the field.

For a moment she looked at him, willing him not to turn away, wanting to raise her leaden hand.

His head tilted slightly and she held her breath. *Be quiet, heart. He'll hear you.*

He raised his hand and though she could not be sure at such a distance, she sensed he was smiling.

Her own hand moved in response. *Higher, Liri! Let him see you're waving, too.*

She watched as he vaulted the gate. She should climb her gate, too. She should walk across the field, meet him half way. But her feet refused to move so she waited until he was within calling distance then whispered, 'Hullo.'

No sound came, but he must have read the moving of her lips because he smiled and said, 'Hullo, Liri.'

She stood unmoving as his pace quickened, catching her breath as he settled his back against her gate, so close to her that had she moved her elbow just half an inch to the left, they would have touched.

Stiffly she followed his gaze across the paddock, searching panic-stricken for something to say. In the end another Liri, the woman who lived inside her, the Liri who dreamed secret dreams and thought secret thoughts spoke for her.

'I – I thought you were married, Gideon.' The words rushed clumsily out. 'I was sure you were.'

'No.' He was still gazing ahead but his body was relaxed, his breathing even. 'There was only ever you.'

'I waited, that night, but you never came. You left

without a word.'

'And so did you, Liri. Without trace, either. No one knew where you'd gone.'

'That was the way I wanted it, the only way there was. I didn't think anyone would care.'

He spun round to face her. He did it so abruptly that she jumped backward.

'Look, we've both got a lot to explain.' They were fencing, skirting around the subject still, as if each was afraid to break the divide yet each wanting desperately to do so. 'We must talk. Now.'

For just a moment the old hurt returned and she heard herself saying, 'Now? After so long it's suddenly urgent?'

She saw the stiffening of his jaw, the sharp sideways moving of his head.

'I deserved that Liri, but at least let me explain?'

'Everything?' she choked. 'Felicity?'

'*Everything.*'

Their closeness was making her dizzy yet she dare not turn her head or their lips would be just a kiss away. They were trembling on the edge of love and she wanted to savour the moment. But most of all, she needed to be sure.

'Can we walk?' she whispered, opening the gate and stepping though. 'Have you time?'

He nodded, and fell into step beside her.

'I'd like to go to Queen's Reach. Tom Cook said the lilies might be out.' Her voice trailed away and she willed him not to touch her. Not yet. Not here.

He nodded, his hands deep in his pockets.

'I'd like to pick some. I want them for a design. I thought I might do a pattern of roses and lilies – maybe call it *Rose Hedge*. I design textiles – did you know?' Why was she babbling on so?

They walked on; past the beech tree underneath which she had wished and across Queen's Reach paddock.

'I got a shock when I realized the house had gone,' she said.

'It was old. Matthew never wanted it. Better it should have gone like that.'

'You don't care, Gideon?' Aghast she turned to look at him directly for the first time. 'It was such a lovely old house.'

'It was cold and draughty and slowly falling down,' he retorted flatly. 'But you could never see fault in it, could you Liri? You loved it far more than we did.'

'I still do. I'm glad there's going to be another Queen's Reach.'

'Yes, it's almost finished. Like to take a look at it?' His voice was softer now.

'I – I only wanted to see if the lilies were out.' Suddenly she was afraid; afraid of the past and of the future, too. But mostly she was afraid of the present and the feelings raging inside her. To go back there with Gideon beside her was asking a great deal.

'You don't remember? It means nothing to you? But of course there's *James darling*. I'd forgotten him!'

His eyes were dark again, his mouth set traplike.

'Don't, Gideon.' It was going wrong again. Soon they would quarrel and all she wanted to do was to tell him she loved him; that she had never stopped loving him. 'Please don't.'

They had reached the old stableyard, full now of builder's litter. Soon, a part of her past would be gone for ever, swallowed up as Pond Cottage had been. Soon her hayloft would be used as a bedroom and someone else would make love there.

'Sorry, Liri. He's none of my business. Eight years is a long time, I suppose. But do you want to look? The builder has made a good job of the conversion. The only stupid thing he did was to get rid of the last of the land. Why ever he tacked those four acres on to Southgate

Lodge I'll never understand.'

'Nor me,' Liri sighed. 'Do you realize they were the original reach of land given to that first Whitaker?' They were speaking calmly again.' 'I – I suppose I might sell them back. If I take a liking to the person who eventually buys this house, I mean.'

'Then you'll be selling them to me, Liri. I'm buying the new Queen's Reach,' he said softly.

'Oh, Gideon. I'm so glad!' Her joy was sincere and obvious.

'Come on.' He held out his hand, smiling again. 'Let's start at the kitchen?'

She placed her hand in his and longing raged through her afresh.

'Gideon – about James . . . .'

'The kitchen,' he said firmly. 'Let's see what you think of it.'

She thought it was wonderful, and said so. 'Wasn't this the tack-room?' she murmured, remembering the smell of leather and saddle soap.

'That's right. They've knocked an extra window in the east wall so it'll get the morning sun.'

Liri gazed at the pine cupboards and the gleaming white Aga and imagined plates of porridge and boiled brown eggs and children around the table.

'How many bedrooms?' she asked automatically.

'Four. And two bathrooms and a boxroom. Be careful on the stairs; the banister isn't fixed yet.'

He led her toward the upstairs rooms and she followed him reluctantly, her boots crunching on wood-shavings.

'Remember this?' He pushed open a door and they stood in a low-ceilinged room with dormer windows on either side.

'Yes.' He was cheating. He shouldn't have brought her here, to the hayloft. She ran her tongue round suddenly-dry lips. Her cheeks flamed hotly and she walked to one of the windows, standing with her back to him, her body shaking. 'It's changed a bit.' She tried to sound flippant.

'You think so?' He was standing behind her now, his hands hard on her shoulders. 'I shall probably have this bedroom for my own. Tell me – shall I be sharing it with a ghost, Liri, or a flesh and blood woman? Will it be just another bedroom or will it be the hayloft, like always?'

He turned her to face him and she closed her eyes and tilted her chin. They were past the point of no return but still she resisted him. She had only to reach out, take his head in her hands as she had always done and abandon her lips to his. He had brought her here purposely and there was nothing to do but surrender.

'Gideon,' she breathed as she gave way to the wanton woman inside her.

Softly his lips touched hers. She felt his breath on her cheek and the hardness of his thighs against her own. Need screamed through her afresh and she relaxed against him, searching with her mouth for his.

'*Damn!*' Somewhere a door banged and she felt the involuntary stiffening of his body. 'Be quiet. Don't move,' he hissed as footsteps sounded in the passage below.

'You there, Mr Whitaker?'

'Up here,' he grated.

Oh, damn, damn, *damn*. Liri let go her breath as Gideon released her abruptly and stepped back. 'It'll be the heifer,' he muttered, a farmer again.

'Flora?' Liri took a deep, steadying breath.

'Yes. She'll have started calving. I'd better go.' They walked across the room and on to the landing. 'Be with you in a minute, Colin,' he called, then smiling ruefully he whispered, 'Well, I suppose it'll keep?'

'Yes.' She was still shaking. 'Tomorrow night? My place?'

'When?'

'About seven.' Her words were little more than a

whisper.

'Seven?' His eyes still held hers. 'Not until then?'

'No.'

He turned abruptly then clattered down the stairs and she walked to the window and watched him go, clutching her stomach, pressing down hard on the rampaging butterflies; loving them, loving the entire world.

Tomorrow. Wonderful tomorrow, at seven . . . .

The first day of May proved to be wayward. It began with a headache, the result, Liri admitted, of a near sleepless night. She had lain awake for most of the time, wanting to lift the phone, to dial Gideon's number and breathe, 'I love you.' But something had held her back. In spite of what had happened a small, niggling fear remained. Nor was she able to settle to work. For all her efforts she was restless and unable to concentrate.

Impatiently she put down her brush, remembering that one of her rose bushes was growing suckers which should be cut away at once and not allowed to grow until Tom Cook's next visit. Relieved to find an excuse, Liri slipped down from her stool, insisting that a break in the garden could do no harm.

Why had she said seven tonight? she fretted. Why not this afternoon or now, even?

Would it always be like this, she mused, taking a sharp knife from the kitchen drawer. Did being suddenly in love again turn your whole world upside-down, make you tearful and happy and restless and jumpy, all at the same time? And why was time passing so slowly? Could it really only be ten o'clock, and if it was, why was she so ravenously hungry?

'There now,' she whispered to the rose bush, carefully cutting away the offending shoots. 'Didn't hurt much, did it?'

She was talking to flowers, now. She might as well tell it to the bees, Liri supposed. Once, when there had been hives at Pond Cottage, Gran had told everything of importance to the tiny creatures.

Liri wished there were bees at Southgate. She could tell them, then.

Listen bees, I'm so in love I can't think straight, but don't tell anyone - not yet!

By midday she had decided it was useless to work on the design and filled in the time instead by polishing and repolishing the furniture and rearranging flowers already arranged to perfection.

Mentally she checked the kitchen. The kettle was filled and a tray set with cups and saucers, just in case Gideon might want tea. In the living-room stood her new brandy glasses, ready to be lifted in a toast to the future.

Liri picked up the mantel clock, shook it, then compared its time with that on her wristwatch.

Irritably she decided against a glass of sherry or a sip of brandy and in the end she washed her hair, wound it in a towel, then sank into a softly-scented bath.

She leaned back frowning, wondering what to wear. The caftan was definitely out. It was too flimsy and soft and the remembered touch of Gideon's hands through its thinness set her heart thumping with remembered ecstasy.

Finally, she surveyed her image in the bedroom mirror and found it entirely displeasing and sensibly safe. Creamy leather pumps, a softly-gathered skirt of fine wool, a cream and coral checked blouse, tied demurely at the neck. Her hair shone, her eyes sparkled nervously, and if her heart didn't stop its terrible thumping she would choke; she really would.

The mantel clock chimed seven. He was late! But had she really expected he would come? Gideon had a long record of broken dates. Even at this moment he could be jetting across the Atlantic, Canada-bound.

The knock on the front door made her jump nervously. Closing her eyes, she forced herself to count slowly to ten before she could muster the courage to open it.

'Liri.' He said her name gently, like a whispered caress.

He was wearing a soft, checked shirt open at the neck, and trousers that emphasized the slimness of his hips.

The tips of her fingers began to tingle and she clenched her hands tightly. She recalled how his hips excited her; how once she had laid possessive hands on their nakedness.

'Come in,' she smiled, marvelling at the evenness of her voice.

He was carrying chocolates and a pink-speckled white orchid. Like a lover come a-courting Liri giggled hysterically inside her. But that was what she needed, really. Gideon must not rush things, much as she longed for him to do so. This time nothing must be allowed to go wrong. There were things to be said, misunderstandings to be straightened out. And she wanted to be courted, old-fashioned though it seemed. She wanted to tease him a little, to flirt, even. This time they must both be absolutely sure.

'Come into the kitchen.'

He followed her without question and watched as she placed the flower in water.

'It's beautiful,' she whispered. 'I've never been given an orchid, before.'

'I phoned York; they delivered it this afternoon,' he smiled.

'Sheer extravagance,' she scolded. 'Are – are you very rich, Gideon?'

'I suppose I am,' he shrugged. 'But what about you, Liri?'

'I'm doing quite well,' she smiled. He obviously didn't know about her award. 'Do you want to see the house?'

How very polite they were being; how well-behaved.

'Later. I came here to talk. About *us*.'

'Yes.' Her mouth had gone dry and she folded her arms tightly to lessen the trembling. Then she flopped inelegantly into a chair and nodded to the sofa-bed opposite. 'Do sit down, Gideon.' She ached for the touch of his hands; longed to feel his mouth on hers, but not yet.

'First let me say I'm sorry, Liri. If what happened hurt you my darling —'

'Hurt me? I waited, Gideon. We were going to tell your father, then tell Gran and Grandpa. You didn't come.' The past had caught up with the present. The flood gates were open and the hurt of years poured out. 'You knew all along I'd be there yet you were miles away, at some airport.'

She jumped to her feet and walked to the window, staring out, seeing nothing. She couldn't bear to look at his face.

'Yes, I knew. But I had to give my word to Father. He'd found out about us, you see.'

'But how?' she whispered dully. 'How could he have known that we were —'

'Lovers?' he supplied grimly. 'Oh, Liri-love, we weren't very discreet. Your grandfather knew, too.'

'No! He couldn't have.'

She flung round to face him, a flush of shame staining her cheeks. Her grandparents had been so straight-laced; Puritan, almost. She sat down heavily again, not trusting her legs to support her.

'Liri, they all knew. They arranged it between them – before things got out of hand, Father said. He played merry hell with me; said you were only a child.'

'I was almost eighteen!'

'I know, but my father said the separation would be good for both of us. He made me give my word I wouldn't get in touch with you for six months. At the end of that time, he said, he'd be satisfied we cared enough to marry. Your grandfather agreed with him.'

'And you expect me to believe that?' Liri gasped. 'It – it's like the plot of a Victorian melodrama.'

'Nevertheless, it's true. The old folks were a bit dramatic, let's face it. I suppose it was the only way they could think of to calm things down. Like I said, they knew we were lovers.'

'It wasn't because I was the gardener's granddaughter – *illegitimate* granddaughter – and you were the squire's son?' The bitterness in Liri's voice was evident.

'Darling. You know that isn't true.'

She clucked impatiently. He was calling her darling and it wasn't fair. She loved him so much, yet she was afraid. There was still eight years of heartache to be explained away. He mustn't call her darling. Not yet.

'I wrote to you, Liri, as soon as I got to Canada. I'd given my word not to, but I was desperate.'

'I didn't get it, Gideon.' Surely Grandpa hadn't kept it from her?

'I realized you hadn't, so I wrote again when Father got ill, telling you I'd be home. But you didn't reply.'

'No. I'd left Pond Cottage by then.'

'But you do believe me, darling? I thought after that you didn't want any more to do with me.'

'I believe you,' she whispered. She *had* to believe him, because any minute now she would fling herself into his arms.

'Tell me about Canada, Gideon,' she prompted huskily.

'Well, I went under protest. Then Matthew wrote to tell me that Father wasn't so well. I started making arrangements to come home, then, because I was determined never to go back. But there were things to be cleared up first – it was about that time I'd found the uranium ore – and I didn't get back to Abbeyfield as quickly as I'd have liked.'

'If only I'd known, Gideon. If only I'd got your letters – one of them, even.'

'I know,' he shrugged. 'Our life seems to have been littered with *if-onlys,* doesn't it? If only I'd known I was going to be rich enough one day to tell Father to go to hell . . . .'

'And when you did come back?'

'You'd gone, Liri. Pond Cottage was empty and they told me at the estate office that you'd handed in the keys and left no forwarding address. I asked everybody but it seems you'd told no one where you were. You could have been at the other side of the world for all I knew. You got on the York bus with two cases, they said, and that was it. It seemed you'd left without trace.'

'That was the way I wanted it to be, Gideon. I'd got a place at Liverpool Polytechnic and vowed that no one was ever going to see Liri Haslington again – not in Abbeyfield, that was. I was so alone; so bitter.' She stopped, hurt throbbing through her. 'Funny, isn't it?' she choked. 'Gran must have known why you left so suddenly; must even have known about that first letter you sent, but she never told me – not so much as a hint. I suppose she'd given up wanting to live, though, after Grandpa died. She just sat there, hardly speaking. If only she'd said. Just one word, and I'd have waited.'

'How you must have hated me.'

'No, Gideon. Not at the time. I was just too numb. I seemed to have lost everything I'd ever known or loved. I hated you afterwards though – or at least I tried to. When I found about Felicity, that was.'

'When was that, Liri?'

'Two years later, when I was a student.' She told him about the dentist's waiting-room and seeing the engagement announcement in the dog-eared society glossy; the shattering realization that he was going to marry someone else. 'I'd gone for a filling and I seemed to remember the dentist asking me if I wanted an injection. I told him I didn't. I wanted it to hurt, you see, but I didn't feel a thing. I don't remember going back to my digs, even. I only know I didn't cry.'

'Oh, my poor darling.' He jumped to his feet, taking her hands in his, pulling her gently against him.

'*No*. Please don't. The old pain was back, and very real. She pushed him away. 'Don't – don't touch me. Not yet. Not until you've told me about – about *her*.'

She walked round to the back of the chair as if to place it between them; to shelter behind it from the force of his love.

'All right – if I must,' he shrugged. 'Felicity was a great girl really, but looking back it was a half-hearted kind of engagement. I'd never looked at her, you see, and imagined her pregnant with my children – not the way I'd looked at you, Liri.'

'So you broke it off?'

'No. She did. One day I called her by your name. It was as simple as that. I called her Liri-love and she blew up, demanded to know about you. So I told her everything and that was the end of our engagement. You can't blame her, really.'

'No. I'd have done the same myself, I shouldn't wonder.'

'So you see, I never forgot you, darling. You were always there like a sad little ghost. You were even there when Felicity was in my arms.'

'Don't, Gideon!'

'You asked me, and I've told you the truth. After Felicity I knew it'd never be any use. I started playing the field. I had all the girls I wanted, but not one of them had your hair or your eyes or felt as you'd felt, in my arms.'

'Oh, Gideon, what are we to do?' The ache inside her had lessened, now. Only her heart was refusing to behave.

'Let's start again, my darling and let's not wait! I want

113

us to be married.'

'When?' she gasped.

'Tomorrow?'

'No! We've got to be sure and I – I want to be courted. I know it sounds old-fashioned, but I want us to take up where we left off so nothing can go wrong, this time.'

'I couldn't agree more, and the sooner we start, the better. Because how much longer I'm going to be able to stand here making atonement for past sins, I don't know. Let's go to Queen's Reach, Liri?'

'No. This time we've got to wait, Gideon. And besides,' she relaxed sufficiently to let a little laugh escape her lips, 'it isn't a hayloft any longer. It's almost a bedroom.'

'Call it what you like, it'll always be the hayloft to me. I want you, Liri.'

'Oh, *why* are you making it so hard? Can't you see, I've got to have time to think, to get used to – to *us*. I thought I'd lost you, you see. I'd accepted it was over. Give me a little time. Let me be absolutely sure.'

She shook her head vehemently, even though her heart cried, but you *are* sure. Since you came back, you've thought of nothing else but Gideon's arms and Gideon's mouth on yours.

'So what d'you think I'm made of, woman? How long am I to be kept dangling?'

They were standing toe to toe, almost, the air between them pulsating with longing.

'For just a little while longer?' Liri begged.

'All right, then. As a matter of fact, I've arranged to go to London tomorrow which is probably just as well. And I'm stopping off at Birmingham on the way back to look at a harvester. It could be Sunday before I'm home – is that enough time for you?'

She nodded, smiling. 'Can we leave it until Sunday afternoon?' She would make an occasion of it she thought, out of the blue. Connie would be there and maybe she could ask Colin McLeod over, too. Suddenly she wanted to share her happiness, have someone there to wish them well. And it would be a lovely surprise for Gideon, she thought with excitement. And she *was* going to tell him she would marry him. The woman inside her wanted to say the words now, but Liri – or was it Roz? demanded that she should wait.

'All right, then. Sunday afternoon it must be. But under protest, mind. Sackcloth and ashes were never my strong suit.' He smiled and tweaked her nose gently. 'Did I tell you I love you, by the way?'

'Not in so many words,' she said softly. 'Now would you like a drink before you go?'

'No thanks. You know what I want.'

'Yes.' She smiled softly, her eyelids half closed. 'But I want us to wait until Sunday. I – I've got a special reason, you see.' Yes, a surprise engagement party definitely appealed to her. 'Get your London trip out of the way then come round on Sunday. About four o'clock?'

'It's just a thought,' he smiled, 'but I don't suppose you'd come to London with me?'

'No. I'm a working girl.' She shook her head, smiling, wishing he didn't look so good it hurt even to look at him.

'Well,' he grinned, 'it was worth a try. But I'm warning you, Liri Haslington, this is the very last time I'll take no for an answer.' She smiled and said nothing, all the while teasing him with her eyes.

'I love you,' he said again. 'Don't I get a kiss – not even a little forgiving one?'

'We-e-ll, you're still officially in the doghouse, Gideon Whitaker,' she smiled, brushing his cheek briefly with her lips.

And I am afraid, she whispered inside her. We mustn't kiss, my darling. If we do, I'm lost.

'Oh, but you'll pay for this!' he exploded.

'Is that a threat sir, or a promise?' she teased, opening

the door.

'Both, so help me,' he grated, reaching for her, holding her so close she was overpowered by the need in him. 'God, how I want you,' he jerked, his mouth searching for hers. 'Come with me to London? I don't want to let you out of my sight.'

Their lips met and his kiss was harsh and demanding. For just a moment her resolve wavered, then she pushed him away.

'Sunday,' she breathed. 'Don't ring or write, meantime. Just come.'

He let go his breath then turned abruptly and she stood there bemused, watching him go, listening until the sound of his footsteps had faded into the night.

'*Idiot!*' she gasped.

Why had she sent him away? Why hadn't she done as she had longed to do; longed for eight lonely years to do? Why hadn't she let him stay, sleep in her arms? Why, why, *why* had she held him at arm's length when every sensuous pulse in her aching body screamed out for him?

But it would all come right, her heart assured her. On Sunday, Connie and Colin would know they were going to be married. This time, nothing would prevent it.

'Darling,' she whispered into the night, 'take care of yourself. I love you so very much . . . .'

Later that night she placed the orchid on the table beside her bed.

I shall carry a bouquet of lilies of the valley and pink roses when we are married, she thought dreamily. And there will be one special orchid in it, too; a pink-speckled white orchid.

She closed her eyes and slept almost at once, to dream of weddings and Gideon; of honeymoons and Gideon; of being in love for ever with Gideon. And when she awoke the orchid was there, to tell her it would all come true.

'I love you, love you, love you,' she murmured. 'Be good

in London and take care. You're so very precious, my dearest love.' Clasping her hands behind her head she stretched her body luxuriously and thought about Sunday. Lovely Sunday, when the whole wide world would know of their love.

'Oh, Gran, Grandpa - everything's wonderful,' she whispered. 'It all came right in the end and I'm so happy. So very *very* happy.

Seven

Liri was relieved when Friday came, for the week had slipped by in a daze of happiness, interspersed with nagging moments of complete disbelief. By some small miracle she had managed to remain at her drawing-board until working sketches of the lily and rose design had been completed and posted off for the manufacturer's approval; relieved that for some of the time at least her head seemed in charge of her heart.

Afternoons had been spent in working on the flower pictures she had faithfully promised Connie would be ready on time. Thank goodness, Liri sighed, laying aside her brush, that water-colour was a reasonably quick medium in which to work.

Lilium wardii. Painstakingly she named the last of the flowers in copperplate script, then initialled the painting with a smile. She always smiled at a completed piece of work; an acknowledgment to the Creator, she supposed; a thank you for the God-given talent which enabled her to produce such work. Such rather good work, she amended, gazing critically at the flamboyant purples and pinks of the flowers.

'Not bad at all, considering —'

Considering she was cross-eyed with happiness, she conceded, slipping down from her high stool.

She sighed again and stretched luxuriously, thinking how utterly sinful it was that any one person could be so happy. Because she *was* happy and so completely contented that if she let herself think about it for too long she became apprehensive again.

Don't let anything spoil it this time, she yearned silently, gazing across the fields to the cottage beyond the beechwood, thinking about Gideon and his suffocating masculinity. She imagined herself pregnant with his child and the sensuous pulses began to beat again. To stand beside him, her body exquisitely ungainly with the evidence of their loving must surely be the most beautiful thing in the world.

The sudden ringing of the telephone hit her like a shock-wave and she descended reluctantly from the soft cloud of her day-dreaming.

'Hullo?' Her voice was husky with longing.

'Darling?'

'Gideon! Where are you? You said you wouldn't ring.'

'I'm still in London and it was *you* who said I shouldn't ring.'

'Is something wrong?' Her heart began to thud.

'No. Only that I'm here and you're there. I'm leaving in a few minutes for Birmingham and I should be back on Sunday morning. By the way, I love you and I want you. I'm giving you fair warning . . . .'

The line went dead before Liri could answer and she closed her eyes as desire shivered through her.

'And I want *you,* my darling,' she whispered. 'I love you so much; so very much.'

And on Sunday they would meet again. By Sunday, everyone would know. And when Connie had left, she and Gideon would talk about their wedding.

'I'm so happy,' she whispered. 'So incredibly, stupidly happy that it can't be true. It just can't.'

As Liri drove to York, though, her emotions were under reasonable control. Connie was coming; the flower paintings had been finished and soon the lights in Woodsman's Cottage would tell her that Gideon had returned.

She was becoming more and more excited about Sunday. Only that morning she had had the most marvellous idea about their wedding.

When Gideon and I are married, she decided with delight, we'll have a marquee on the lawn at Queen's Reach.

She wondered why she had not thought of it before. A late-June wedding perhaps, with a choir and a peal of bells and the reception in a marquee smelling of canvas and flowers and trodden grass.

She shook her head clear of remembered fantasies and left her car in the station car-park. Her happiness would be noticed, of course. Connie missed nothing, she acknowledged as she pushed coins into the platform-ticket machine. And she was late, she fretted, slamming up the steps and across the bridge, arriving breathless at the platform as the train from King's Cross pulled in.

'Well now,' Connie greeted her. 'It's pretty obvious who's got herself sorted out at long last.'

'We-e-ll, not quite,' Liri wrinkled her nose. 'I don't know why, but for some reason I played a little hard-to-get. Gideon's been away all week, but I shall say yes when he asks me again. Nothing's changed, Con. We still love each other.' The colour flamed in her cheeks. 'It – it shows, I suppose?'

'It does and it suits you and I'm very glad about it – if it hasn't affected your work, that is.'

'It hasn't,' Liri grimaced. 'After a bit of a struggle I finished the pictures you wanted and sent some sketches to Hathaway-Paige.'

'Good. Y'know, I've been really looking forward to visiting again – bought myself some gum-boots, as a matter of fact. I've got to admit that your Abbeyfield could very easily grow on me. Any news of Flora, by the way?'

'Flora? Oh, the little heifer.' Liri's cheeks flamed again as she remembered the bedroom at Queen's Reach and the farm manager's untimely interruption. 'N-no, I've heard nothing, but you can ask Colin McLeod on Sunday. He's coming to tea, by the way; thought you might like to talk about hay and Herefords,' she teased, a fresh surge of happiness wrapping her round like a scented summer breeze. 'But let's get home.'

Lovely home; lovely Abbeyfield; lovely, lovely world.

Later that evening, when they had eaten, Liri insisted that Connie should go out.

'I'll do the washing-up,' she smiled, 'and you know you're longing to try out your new wellingtons.'

'Well, I might just take a quick look at your fields. And maybe I'll be able to get news of Flora. Sure you don't mind?'

'Out! And get some good country air into your lungs.'

Liri commanded, surveying the litter of pans and plates with near affection. Even washing-up had ceased to be a chore. But being in love did strange things to people. Being in love was — ? She sighed ecstatically. Being in love was so wonderful that right now it wasn't possible to find words to describe it.

She sighed again, squirted soap into the sink and flatly refused to allow herself one more daydream. By the time

Connie returned, she told herself sternly, the kitchen must be tidy again and the coffee percolating on the stove top. And it was.

'Meet anyone?' she asked casually when Connie clumped back into the kitchen.

'Er – only Colin McLeod. Flora's OK, by the way. Colin let me see her calf and he's called Hamish though he's got a far grander name on his pedigree, of course.'

'Oh, of course.' Liri hid a smile. 'So do you want *my* news, now? I'd have thought you'd be bursting to discover what went wrong, all those years ago.'

'I do love, and I am,' Connie said quietly, glancing at the brandy glasses on the coffee table. 'I take it there's something to drink to?'

'There is. But wait till I tell you! You'll never believe it not in a thousand years.'

'Try me, Roz. Right now I think I'm in a mood to believe almost anything.'

Cryptic words, and lost on Liri. Which was a pity, really, because had she looked closer she might have recognized the expression in the eyes of her friend as being distinctly remote. And had that happened, it would have set her wondering how anyone except Colin McLeod, of course – could become so dreamy-eyed over a Hereford bull-calf.

'Now listen to this, Con,' she insisted, and Connie Davies smiled remotely, and listened.

'Well, that's what happened, and isn't it *incredible?*' Liri finished breathlessly. 'Can you believe it? Can you imagine such melodrama? Gideon being ordered away like that, I mean, and in disgrace almost. Things like that shouldn't happen any more.'

'Seems they do, though, in Abbeyfield. But didn't you warn me this village is years behind the times? Maybe

Gideon accepted his father's ultimatum for your sake, Roz. And your grandparents must've been a bit upset when they discovered how far things had gone between you. Remember they were two generations removed and you must both have seemed a bit – well —' Connie shrugged. 'But I suppose you'll be thinking about weddings and things, now?'

'I hope so. I want us to be married, Con. The living together bit wouldn't go down at all well in Abbeyfield and besides, I want children.'

'Makes sense,' Connie smiled. 'And to think that last week at this time —'

'You'd just dropped your lovely bombshell,' Liri supplied. "How will I ever be able to thank you?'

'Don't try dear. You can't,' she grinned impishly. 'But how about that toast? Let's drink to falling in love, shall we?'

'I think I'm going to cry,' Liri choked.

'No you're not. You're going to think about all the tomorrows.'

Connie poured brandy into the glasses. 'You're going to marry your Gideon and live happily ever after. I absolutely insist.'

'Yes,' Liri smiled tremulously, lifting her glass, sniffing inelegantly. 'I am – aren't I?'

And she would stop this lovely weeping in just a minute. She really would.

Saturday passed in an upheaval of cake-making, polishing and dusting, and the arranging of flowers.

'And that,' Liri gasped eventually, 'leaves only scones to be made and sandwiches to be cut and I can do that in the morning.'

She took a shuddering breath and looked absently across the garden. Night was stealing in from the meadows and white narcissi glowed dimly in the dusky half-light. Already the garden was responding to Tom Cook's ministrations and now it seemed as if it knew that tomorrow was special, Liri thought, and was putting on a proud show.

'Do you realize this will be my first party, Con? My first real party ever? And can you believe that no one in Abbeyfield has asked me yet what went wrong between Gideon and me, though some of them must be bursting to know?'

She paused for breath. She was so jumpy. She really must calm down.

'Well, if all goes to plan they'll not have much longer to wait,' Connie smiled.

'Yes, and I'm so happy. Oh, I know I keep saying it, but I can't help myself. I keep thinking I'm dreaming and soon I'll wake up and —'

'You aren't dreaming,' Connie interrupted the breathless flow. 'Take a look at Woodsman's Cottage.'

Liri followed the pointing finger with her eyes and recognized the glow of lamplight from the windows of Gideon's cottage.

He was back early. The trembling began again and she hugged herself tightly. Gideon was safely home and tomorrow would be the most wonderful day of her life.

'I don't know about you, but I'm shattered.' Connie slumped into an armchair. 'Like a coffee?'

'No thanks. I feel more like a shower. And my hair must be full of cooking smells. Think I'll wash it now in case things get a bit hectic in the morning.'

But really, Liri admitted, she needed to be alone with her happiness and closing her eyes she lifted her face to the water. And she needed to touch her nakedness; to gentle her hands over every part of her body, feel its hollows and curves and know that tomorrow night Gideon would find pleasure in it. She was tired of waiting, she sighed. She wanted, *needed,* to belong again, to turn back the years and be that other Liri, crazy with love and longing. She had been alone and unloved too long. She wanted Gideon *now.*

The remembered scent of hay invaded her nostrils and every wanton pulse in her yearning body remembered the way it had been.

We wasted so much time, she thought, briefly sad; lost so much loving.

'Hey, Roz! Gideon just phoned.' Connie's voice came dimly from behind the shower curtain. 'I told him you were in the bathroom.'

'Oh, no! Did he say he'd ring again?'

'No. He said not to disturb you. Said it would keep until tomorrow. He'll see you at four as you arranged, he said.'

At four, Liri pondered. Eighteen hours away. A whole lifetime away. Should she ring him back or should she force herself to eke out the hours until he came?

She remembered the red bicycle and decided to wait out those last hours. And when eventually he came, their eyes would meet and there would be no need for question or answer.

She wrapped her hair in a towel and shrugged on her bathrobe.

'Think I'd like a drink,' she smiled, padding barefoot into the sitting-room, pouring a glass of sherry.

It should have been champagne, of course. She felt so high, so heady, that only champagne could have matched her mood. She was still as taut as a coiled spring. Soon, she would explode. She would lift off like a rocket and be lost for ever among the stars.

She drew aside the curtain and saw Gideon's lights burning more brightly through the completeness of the night, loving him until it was like an exquisite pain in her breast.

Only eighteen hours to wait. Eighteen long, lovely maddening hours and then they would meet again, their lips would touch, and the whole world would know.

Liri was glad she awoke early, because to have wasted even a minute of so wonderful a day would have been unforgivable. She was placing the last of the scones to bake when the back-door knocker sounded loudly through the house.

Gideon? She flung open the door to find Colin McLeod standing there, permitting herself a small smile as she realized that this time, had he asked again for her land, she would have said, 'Yes, of course!' without another moment's hesitation. But this time the farm manager was carrying gifts.

'Cream, Miss Haslington. Compliments of Keeper's Lodge Farm and – er – good morning, Miss Davies,' he murmured as Connie yawned her way down the stairs, fastening her dressing-gown as she walked.

'Morning,' she mumbled. 'Stay for a coffee and tell me how Hamish is getting along.'

'Hamish is just fine.' The blue eyes glowed. 'We have a real champion there.'

Liri suppressed a giggle and placed a mug of coffee in Connie's grasp, marvelling how the mention of a week-old calf could bring so much animation to such usually guarded eyes.

'And Flora?'

'She's fine, too. A grand wee lady.'

Liri opened the fridge, shaking with noiseless laughter. Had anyone told her that one day she would be standing in her own kitchen, listening to Connie Davies discussing cows and calves with a rigid-faced Scotsman, she would never have believed it. Any minute now she would laugh out loud at the unrealness of it all; at the unbelievable magic of this day. Either that, she thought shakily, or she would weep. Laughter or tears – it didn't matter. She was as high a kite, jumpy as a kitten, crazily in love. And tonight the years would roll away and Liri Haslington would be eighteen again. And the scent of newly-cut hay would lull her senses as Gideon's lips found hers. Tonight. Exquisite, enchanted, tonight.

The afternoon sun dazzled, the garden smiled and the laburnums and lilacs nodded their approval.

On the sitting-room table stood glasses and bottles of sherry and elderflower wine. Beside them lay sandwiches and cakes and a trifle thick with Keeper's Lodge cream. On the mantel the fingers of the clock stood at four.

Liri looked out across the garden, straining her eyes for the sight of Gideon's car. Then checked the clock again and though she knew she looked good – well, maybe just another peep in the mirror?

She gazed critically. Her dress was of palest green silk with matching shoes in soft leather; her face was paler than usual, her eyes large and far too bright. She still looked like a *liriconfancy,* she thought disparagingly, then closed her eyes briefly, sending her love winging out and away.

I'm happy, she whispered from her heart. *We're together again, Gideon and I.* It seemed only right that Gran and Grandpa should know.

'That's the scones buttered,' Connie sighed, handing the plate to Liri. 'And who do you know who's got a Spitfire?'

'*Spitfire?*'

'Car, lovey. A little red job. It's just come up the lane.'

'Up *my* lane?' Liri frowned.

The red car certainly wasn't Gideon's. She walked to the window and squinted out. And then she saw him and her body stiffened with horror.

Oh, no. Soundlessly her lips formed the plea. Not *today?*

The scones spilled to the floor; the plate slipped from her shaking hand and rolled to a halt beneath the table.

He was walking up the path with a woman at his side. He did it dramatically, almost demanding to be watched. He did it, damn him, like it was a first night and he was taking a curtain-call. She heard his knock, then stood frozen, waiting for the confrontation.

'Roz, my darling.' His eyes flicked over the table. 'Such a welcome. You must have known I was coming.'

'James,' she choked as he drew her toward him and laid his mouth possessively on hers.

She wanted to tell him he wasn't expected, that he wasn't welcome, either, but she could say nothing.

Then he released her, smiling enigmatically and as she lowered herself into a chair she heard Connie's *'Hell and damnation!'* from a million miles distant.

'Nothing to say, my darling? But it's my fault, I suppose,' James smiled indulgently. 'I should have warned you but I couldn't resist surprising you. And let me introduce Verna. She's come up with us.'

'Us?' Liri repeated woodenly.

'*Us.* The television people. Don't say you've forgotten *Night of the Hawkes?* We're here on location for a week and Verna's come along for the ride – and maybe a teeny part, if she's a good girl.'

Liri took the extended hand and it was cold, like her own.

Verna Reid smiled, her eyes guarded. 'So this is your wayward fiancée, James?' she murmured.

Fiancée? Panic screamed through Liri and she looked around her like a trapped animal.

'You'll want a drink, James?'

Liri sensed rather than heard Connie taking charge, shepherding the usurpers to the table.

'Oh my dear, do look? Elderflower wine. How *absolutely quaint,'* Verna drawled.

'Quaint it may be,' came Connie's scathing retort, 'but a couple of those taken at a gallop could blow the top of your head off, ducky.'

'Really?' Verna's eyebrows shot upward. 'What are we drinking to, James? Something special?'

I don't like her, Liri thought wildly. I don't want her here, nor James. Especially not James.

'Of course we're drinking to something special,' James cried, and Liri closed her eyes.

Oh, but he was always the actor; each word clear and resonant and right up to the gallery, he always boasted.

'Please listen!' He beckoned for attention with eloquent hands. He was even good at beckoning too, Liri thought dully. He did it like a benign god, gathering in his followers. This was to be my lovely day and he's ruined it, she thought despairingly

'Please join us in a toast?' James smiled, drawing Liri to her feet, resting a possessive arm on her shoulders, pulling her close.

'Stop it, James!' Connie hissed. 'Nobody's going to drink to anything!'

Liri stiffened. James was smiling his lovely smile again. He did it so perfectly that at times even she had been deceived by it. Times past, that was. Now, she had only to go back to that Sunday afternoon in Connie's flat; recall the harshness of his mouth and the thinly-disguised need in his eyes. And remember, she thought coldly, that he would have taken her without love.

'Oh, but we are, my dear Constance. I'm tired of keeping it a secret. It's time everyone knew that Roz and I are going to be married,' he murmured.

Without love, Liri asserted silently. Her cheeks flamed with remembered shame and slowly the stupor began to leave her.

No! she wanted to cry. It isn't true! We're not engaged; not now – not ever!

She wanted to say it; she would have done, but the words coiled themselves into a tight, hard ball in her throat and stayed unspoken as she followed Connie's stricken gaze. She did it without turning her head, moving only her eyes, sliding them snakelike to the open door where Gideon stood.

A gasp of dismay escaped her and she knew already that he had heard. The eyes that met hers were dark with anger; the lips she had longed for were stiff with distaste. This was not her love. The man who stood there vibrated with contempt and then, as if the sight of her was repugnant to him, he turned abruptly and walked away.

'Gideon!' Her voice came at last in a harsh cry. 'Wait. Please wait!'

Cold with shock she pushed past Colin, wrenching open the door to see Gideon disappear round the corner of the house. And so great was his fury that it wasn't until they were almost at Queen's Reach that she caught up with him.

'Please listen!' She clutched at his arm and he stopped abruptly and hurled round to face her. *'Please?'* she begged. 'I don't know how much you heard or what you thought –'

'I heard enough.' His words were rough with derision. 'And what I thought doesn't bear repeating. But you must be really pleased with yourself, Liri. You waited eight years to do it, and you've finally got your own back! Don't ring from London, you said. Don't make love to me; wait until Sunday? You even set the time for the *denouement,* didn't you?'

'Gideon, *listen,*' Liri hissed through clenched teeth.

'The hell I will! You've had your fun, now you listen to *me!* I'm thinking back, Liri, to what we said the other night and it's only just dawned on me that you never said you loved me; never actually *said* the words. But you were stringing me along, weren't you; playing with me like a fish on the end of a line; waiting for the right moment? I phoned you last night the minute I got home, and —'

'But I was having a shower,' Liri protested, 'and you said not to ring you back.'

'Maybe so – but I hoped you would. I even, in my stupidity, thought you might come over to Woodsman's. God! How you must have enjoyed thinking about me waiting there!'

'No Gideon, that isn't true,' she gasped. 'Discovering you weren't married was a shock and I knew before I said I still loved you that I had to be sure of my feelings. I *did* want to phone, though; just whisper that I loved you. But somehow I wanted to keep it, too – wait until Sunday like we'd said. I was – well, savouring the moment, I suppose. Can't you understand?'

A pain tore through her. Dear, sweet heaven, how she loved him.

'I understand perfectly. You wanted to keep it until *he* was there and it was my humiliation you wanted to savour, wasn't it? Well, I congratulate you. You succeeded brilliantly, Liri. It was a masterly piece of strategy. You know, I'd completely forgotten *James-darling*.'

'Don't!' Her new-found happiness was slipping away from her, and now she was cold with fear. 'Please don't!' She was shaking so much she could hardly stand. 'I can explain if only you'd listen!'

'What I saw needs no explanation. And might I too add my congratulations, my dear? Sorry I have no glass to raise, but I hope you'll both have all the happiness you deserve. In fact I *know* you will. You and that gesticulating Narcissus deserve each other!'

Impatiently he tried to brush aside her hand, but she held on tightly. He *must* listen to her. She would make

132

him. For a moment they gazed into each other's eyes then willing her voice to be calm Liri whispered, 'Darling, I beg you to hear me out. I give you my word —'

'Your word means nothing to me any longer, I'm afraid. Let's forget the whole sordid episode, shall we? I should have realized you'd have changed. It was Liri I loved and remembered all those years but Liri's gone and I don't much like the vindictive woman she's become. Sorry, but that's the way it is.'

Liri shook her head, gazing into the narrowed eyes, trying desperately to find some small chink she might pierce with one last plea. But his face was impersonal as a slab of stone and his eyes were hard and pitiless.

'Have you nothing to say to me?' she whispered.

'Only goodbye,' he said quietly. 'And when you're in *James-darling's* arms, when he's making love to you, Liri, try to forget that once I loved you, too. And try to forget *this!*'

He pulled her to him so suddenly that there was no escaping and his mouth found hers with a harshness that shocked her. She held herself rigid, trying to free her arms but it was as if his kiss had padlocked even her senses. Then slowly, gratefully, she relaxed her body and lay limp against him, returning the fervour of his kiss. His grasp slackened and she reached up and entwined her arms around his neck, pulling him to her again so he should feel the urgent pulsating of her body, let it say the words he denied her.

'Gideon,' she choked as his hands gentled her thighs, moaning softly as he kissed the hollow at her throat and whispered his lips over her cheeks, her eyelids.

He wanted her still! her heart exulted. Soon, his anger would die and he would listen to her. And she would beg him to take her to Woodsman's, to make love to her *now*. There would be no doubts, then. And afterwards, a long time afterwards, they would promise never to quarrel again.

'Oh, my love.' Her knees weakened as his hand cupped her breast, burning through the thin silk of her dress, causing her nipples to harden with wanton pleasure. 'I can explain.'

'Yes, of course you can!' Violently, cruelly, he released her. He did it so abruptly that she staggered and almost fell. 'That was to remember me by,' he hissed, pushing away her clinging arms. 'To remember when you're making love to *him*. Enjoy him if you can, Liri, but know I shall be there each time he takes you. I promise you I shall haunt each kiss and caress.'

He stopped, his chest heaving with unsuppressed passion, then turning contemptuously he strode toward the stableyard, vaulting the fence without a backward glance.

'Gideon!' she cried harshly, but her words were lost to him.

Shaking and shocked she realized there was nothing she could do. Somehow she must pull herself together. For the rest of the day she must force herself to live out the nightmare. But tonight, when they had both had time to think, she would go to Woodsman's Cottage. She would bang on his door, sit on his doorstep all night if she had to, but she would make him listen. And until then, she resolved, forcing herself to breathe slowly and deeply, she must go back to Southgate and do what she could to put things right.

She would, she considered, make light of it all; insist that James was a tease who couldn't resist his little joke. And if he had any sense he would accept that he had failed again, and laugh with her. She would soon sort it out. Colin would hear her denial. Soon, Gideon would realize it was only him she loved.

Tilting her chin, straightening her shoulders, she walked back to the little house but with each faltering step a little of her new-found resolve deserted her.

It's gone wrong again, whispered her common sense. You shouldn't have prevaricated. You should have gone with him to London, like he asked you. But you wanted to be courted, to be sure. Why did you drag your feet when all you wanted was to love and be loved? Can you blame him for jumping to the wrong conclusions?

Dejectedly she trailed up the path, closing the door quietly behind her. Wearily she paused outside the open door of the sitting-room, listening to the fury in Connie's voice.

'You idiot, James! You're better than anyone I know at opening your mouth and putting your foot in it! Do you realize what you've done? *Do you?*'

'I'm not in the habit of joking about marriage; my own marriage in particular,' came the frosty retort. 'I meant what I said. I intend to marry Roz.'

'Then you're going about it in a very peculiar way. Won't you ever get it into your conceited head that she doesn't want you?' Connie hissed.

'Er – pardon me?' Liri heard Verna Reid's theatrical yawn. 'Sorry, James, but include *me* out of this particular little drama. I'll wait in the car and if you want a lift back to the digs you'd better hurry. I've got things to do.'

Liri waited, eyes closed in despair, until the tapping of Verna's heels outside could no longer be heard. Then she took a deep breath and entered the room.

For a while she found it impossible to speak. Dully she gazed around her at the mockery of plates of uneaten food and the untouched dish of trifle; longing to take it in her shaking hands and hurl it through the open window. But instead she walked zombielike across the floor and sank into a chair.

'Please do as Miss Reid asks, James,' she whispered. 'I want you to leave.'

It was as if the events of the past few minutes had

drained her of all emotion, leaving her shocked and almost incapable of coherent speech.

Disbelieving, she looked at the mantel clock. Just ten minutes. Was that really all the time it had taken to shatter her life so completely?

'Now hang on, Roz. It's about time we got things straightened out once and for all,' James demanded. 'You've been blowing hot and blowing cold for far too long. For some utterly inexplicable reason you suddenly decide to tear up your roots and come to live in this deserted hole. All right, you've had your fun and now it's got to stop. I'm asking you again to marry me and I'll go on asking until you say yes!'

'And I am saying no,' Liri flung, her eyes fixed trancelike on the clock face. 'And I'll go on saying no until *you* accept it. So thank you James, but no, no, *no* . . . .'

'You heard what the lady said,' Connie hissed as Verna's car-horn blared. 'Better go James, or you'll miss out on your lift.'

'We're filming at Hazlebank Castle.' James ignored Connie completely, directing his reply to the back of Liri's chair. 'I'm staying at the White Hart, in Hazlebank village. Call me, Roz?'

But Liri did not answer. She knew only that her lovely day had ended in heartache.

'Where's Colin?' she whispered, when she and Connie were alone.

'Gone. He left a little while after Gideon. Said something about helping with the milking.'

'I see,' Liri whispered. So much for her public denial. So much for James' little joke and the good laugh they'd all have.

'Oh, Con.' She covered her face with hands that shook. 'Gideon wouldn't listen. I tried to explain, begged him to hear me out, but he wouldn't.'

If only James hadn't picked that precise time at which

to blunder back into her life. If only Gideon had arrived earlier or much, much later; if only he'd listened

Our life seems to be littered with if-onlys.

It was only then that Liri realized her lips still hurt from the impassioned fury of their parting kiss and it was then she surrendered to the raging grief inside her and sobbed as if her heart would never be whole again.

Eight

'**M**ood over, then?'
    'Mood over.' Liri dabbed at her eyes, blew her nose loudly and took a shuddering gulp of air. 'I'm all right now, truly I am.'

'That's my girl,' Connie smiled. 'So why don't we make a start on this mess? I'm catching a later train tonight, by the way, so I can give you a hand. Colin said he'd run me to the station – we arranged it on Friday night, as a matter of fact.'

'But I can take you,' Liri protested.

'Sure you can. But won't you be going to Gideon's place? The way I see it, the sooner you get yourselves sorted out, the better.'

'I know,' Liri whispered. 'I lost him before because of my stiff-necked stupidity and I won't let it happen again.'

'Fine. But go easy!' Connie frowned. 'He was really steamed-up when —'

'Oh, no. No more pussyfooting,' Liri jerked. 'I love

Gideon. I always have and where he's concerned I've no pride left. And when I've seen him I'll straighten things out with James – once and for all!'

'No, Roz. If you'll take my advice you'll steer clear of James for the moment. Oh, I know he shouldn't have done what he did,' Connie hastened when Liri opened her mouth to protest, 'but you really can't blame him for trying to pull a fast one. You *did* keep him dangling.'

'I know, and you're right. You always are. It's one of the things about you I can't stand.' Liri glanced in the mirror then turned shuddering away. 'Heavens! Look at my face? Why can't I cry beautifully?'

'Because you're you and you never do anything by halves. But let's make a start, shall we?' Hands on hips Connie regarded the plates of uneaten food. 'I suppose I could take some of this back with me, but it's a pity you haven't got around to buying a deep-freeze.'

'The trifle, you mean?'

'Mm. Oh well, I suppose you could always have it fried for breakfast?'

'Oh, Con.' Liri collapsed giggling on to a chair. 'I *do* love you.'

'Thanks. I'm kind of attached to you too, in spite of your troublesome gentleman friends. So how about taking off the glad-rags and giving your face a splash under the cold tap?'

Suddenly Liri felt much better. And it wasn't the end of the world, she insisted as she dabbed dry her face then pulled on jeans and a shirt. There had been a misunderstanding, but when she and Gideon had calmed down they would sort things out. They were in love, weren't they? It was bound to come right, in the end.

'It *must*,' she whispered to her wide-eyed mirror image. 'I couldn't go through it all again. I couldn't.'

* * *

When she heard the braking of a car in the lane outside, Liri hurried downstairs, heart thumping. But it was the farm manager who stood at the kitchen door.

'Mr McLeod – do come in?' She forced a smile to her lips, marvelling that her voice should sound so unconcerned.

'I came to see if I could help in any way. Perhaps I could take the cleaner over the carpet?' He gazed pointedly at the remains of the buttered scones.

'*You?* Goodness, I can't imagine —' She stopped abruptly, blushing bright red. 'I'm sorry. I – I shouldn't have said that. I'm not quite myself, I'm afraid.'

'I think I understand,' he returned gravely. 'I suppose it isn't every day a lady becomes – er – engaged?'

'You're right,' Liri whispered, grateful for his understanding. 'It came as something of a shock, as a matter of fact.'

'And utterly without foundation,' Connie added brusquely. 'James Howard *will* have his little joke.'

'Only this time the joke misfired?'

'Full marks for diplomacy,' Connie nodded. 'But I suppose it'll all get sorted out.' She glanced meaningfully at Liri.

'Yes. I – I'd thought about going over to Woodsman's,' Liri faltered. 'Later on, maybe.'

'Then might I make a suggestion?' Colin McLeod's face broke into a rare smile. 'Mr Whitaker intends eating out tonight. I called on him before I came here and he was on the phone, making a booking at the Coach House Inn. A table for two, I gathered. At seven.'

'Well, there you are, Roz.' Connie pursed her lips. 'Looks like you're about to be offered the olive-branch.'

'You think so?' Liri gasped. 'Oh, it was all so stupid. I could wring James's neck.'

'I thought we'd agreed to forget that gentleman,' Connie reminded. 'Why don't you give Gideon a ring? After all, it wouldn't hurt to meet him halfway.'

'No, Con. I've made up my mind to go to Woodsman's.
I'd rather do it that way.'

'Please yourself, lovey, but get a move on. You don't
have a lot of time – not if you want to catch him before he
phones you, that is.'

Connie was so sensible, Liri acknowledged later as she
carefully repaired the ravages of her weeping. It was
obvious Gideon was regretting his outburst; had probably
even intended Colin to drop a discreet hint about the
reservation at the restaurant. Right now, she pondered,
he could be feeling distinctly apprehensive and extremely
sorry for his outburst. There could even be a pink-
speckled white orchid awaiting her at that table for two,
she thought longingly.

But she must hurry. She must get to Woodsman's
Cottage before he picked up the phone to call her. He
must be in no doubt that she too had been prepared to
make the first move.

'Sure you can manage, Con?' Liri took her car-keys from
their hook.

'Of course I can. Just get yourself sorted out, that's all I
ask.'

'But your train? I feel so guilty.'

'I'm perfectly capable of boarding a train. And Colin's
running me to the station.'

'Bless you.' Liri kissed her friend warmly. 'I'll give you
a ring later – let you know how things go. Slam the door
behind you when you leave.'

It was not until she was driving down Keeper's Lodge
road that Liri remembered she had not thanked Colin
McLeod. He was rather nice, she was becoming forced to
admit. Dour, but dependable. Connie seemed to like him,
too.

She would be nicer to him in future, Liri decided,
remembering the awful things she had blamed him for.

Such a fuss, she admitted, over four acres of land. But she would let Gideon have them. Her fields would go back to Queen's Reach, where they really belonged. To the new Queen's Reach, where she would live with Gideon when they were married. And they *would* be married, in spite of James's mischief-making.

She stopped the car outside Woodsman's Cottage, glanced briefly in the driving mirror, then ran quickly up the path.

'Funny,' she frowned, when there was no answer to her knock, and pushing open the letter-box she called Gideon's name. After which she walked completely around the house, peering in at windows, satisfying herself that he really was not there.

'But of course!' she laughed with delight. He had already left. Having first established that Colin knew his precise whereabouts, he had gone alone to the restaurant, sure in the knowledge that she would follow.

Liri smiled indulgently, did an amazingly efficient turn in the narrow lane and headed for the Coach House, her heart beating joyously.

I love you, Gideon Whitaker, she whispered inside her, and nothing you do will ever change me. Nothing in the world, my stubborn darling. Nothing in this whole, wide world.

The reception clerk at the Coach House Inn confirmed that Mr Whitaker had indeed booked a table. What was more, she was almost sure he had arrived and was waiting in the lounge.

'He said he was expecting a guest,' she smiled. 'Shall I let him know you've arrived, or would you like to find your own way?' She indicated the direction of the lounge with a nod of her head. 'Second on the left, madam – the double glass door.'

Liri thanked her and rewarded her with a brilliant smile.

But first the cloakroom – just to be sure she was back to normal. She was wearing the cream and coral outfit again, and it suited her, she decided. This afternoon's pale green silk was very beautiful of course, but Liri doubted she would ever wear it again without feeling discomfort.

The hand that held the bright coral lipstick was shaking and she closed her eyes briefly and willed herself to be calm.

It's all perfectly straightforward, she insisted silently. You go down the passage and enter the lounge – having first ascertained where Gideon is sitting. Then you will smile and walk up to him and say, 'Hullo, darling,' like it's the most normal thing in the world; like nothing at all happened this afternoon. That's all you have to do.

Breathing slowly and carefully she walked down the passage, hesitating briefly outside the double glass doors to silently admonish her heart for beating so loudly. Then fixing a smile on her lips she stepped inside.

She very quickly saw Gideon. He was sitting directly opposite the doors on a long, low sofa and in that one second of recognition she took in his lean, tanned face, the expensively-cut dinner jacket, the absolute masculinity of him. And in that same moment she felt the colour drain from her cheeks, for beside him sat a woman who lifted her glass to his and smiled intimately into his eyes.

Verna Reid? But it *couldn't* be! How could they possibly know each other? She had travelled north with James, so how could she now be sitting beside Gideon and drinking champagne as though she had every right to be there?

I shall be sick, Liri thought. If I don't get out of here I shall be very, very sick.

She stumbled into the fresh air and somehow managed to unlock the door of her car and sink shaking behind the wheel.

Verna Reid and Gideon? It was incredible. And why? *How?*

She sat there, icy cold and shocked and it was a long time before she was able to turn the key in the ignition and drive away.

Verna Reid and Gideon? The question beat unmercifully in her head. It just wasn't possible . . . .

The little house was quiet and deserted when Liri returned and she shivered as she picked up Connie's note.

Thanks for an interesting weekend, she read. *Ring me?*

She looked at the mantel clock. Connie wouldn't be home yet and besides, what would be the point now in ringing?

I went to the Coach House, Con, and you were right. Gideon *did* intend me to follow him. And there's only one thing I have to be glad about. I was lucky. He didn't see me. He didn't have the pleasure of seeing my humiliation.

No, Liri acknowledged as she laid a match to the kindling in the grate. Gideon had been too taken up with Verna Reid to take notice of anyone else. They had been sitting close; much, much too close, she thought angrily. Their thighs had touched and Gideon's arm lay along the back of the sofa in an intimate, possessive manner.

How could he? Liri demanded. How could he, when only last night it was me he loved?

He'd see her at four, he told Connie. Like they'd arranged, he'd said. Yet now he was treating her with contempt, kissing her roughly, slamming out of her life. *Again.*

Liri closed her eyes at the memory of it. Cruel though it had been, that kiss had evoked desire in her. It did not matter what he did, she admitted dully, she would never stop wanting him.

And Gideon loved her too, she thought as pain sliced through her. Tonight, for some reason, he had taken another woman out to dinner. Perhaps he had been angry and smarting with imagined humiliation and maybe even now he was regretting his rashness and longing for the evening to end.

We love too deeply, Liri sighed. We hurt each other too easily.

She recalled the night she had waited and her hopeless tears as Grandpa took her in his arms. They had both been too proud to give in, Liri frowned. It never occurred to Gideon to disobey his father – apart from writing to her, of course, and it never entered her head that any explanation existed other than that he had left her without as much as one word of goodbye.

Stiff-necked and foolish, that's what they'd been, and it was happening all over again. I'm condemning Gideon out of hand when all I have to do is pick up the phone and say, 'I love you, my darling.'

The evening sun slanted through the window and tinted the wall to gold. And it shone on the brass fork that hung beside the hearth, evoking memories.

Hot, buttered toast and mugs of tea beside Nanny's hearth. They had been grateful for every moment together then, yet now, just as everything was coming right, they were tearing each other into pieces.

Slowly she walked over to the window, gazing across the meadow and beyond the beechwood to where Woodsman's Cottage lay half-hidden. It was early, yet, but when Gideon returned she would see his light and know that the time had come to pick up the phone.

She loved him too much, she admitted. She had lost him once because she was too proud even to try to get in touch with him, but she wouldn't make the same mistake again. Neither James with his subterfuge nor Verna Reid with all her brittle charm could keep them apart.

Immediately a light showed in Woodsman's Cottage she would gulp down her pique and beg Gideon to see her. Pride was a luxury she could no longer afford.

It was almost midnight before Gideon's upstairs light shone through the darkness.

'At last!' Liri gasped, snatching up the phone, running her tongue round suddenly-dry lips. 'Oh! Wouldn't you know it!'

His number was engaged and she shook her head impatiently. Then she smiled, relieved. He was ringing *her*. She should have known he would.

Frowning, she replaced the receiver. Should she await his call or —?

Snatching up her coat she slammed the front door behind her. Already too much time had been wasted. Nor would she take the car, she decided, as she ran down Meadowsweet Lane. By the time she opened and closed doors and gates she could be there on foot; especially if she took a short-cut across the fields. It wasn't too dark. The sky was full of stars and once her eyes became accustomed to the night, she would make better time.

The beech tree loomed ahead and Liri remembered the wish she had made there, wondering if she should stop and make another? She shook her head, and ran on. The time for wishing was over. Tonight, without any preamble, she would tell Gideon she loved him. Immediately he opened the door she would say it and then they would take it from there.

Climbing the fence she arrived at the river-path. It hadn't taken long, she thought as she slowed her step and forced herself to breathe deeply. The light beckoned and her heart began to thud. She stopped, and closed her eyes.

This time, if he asks me to, I shall stay, she whispered

inside her. I prevaricated before and it was crazy when all the time I was longing to be loved again. Tonight I shall say, 'I love you, Gideon. Please let me explain.' And he'll understand – I know he will and tell me he loves me, too.

She opened her eyes abruptly, gazing hypnotized at the bedroom light and her heart began to beat faster.

'It isn't the hayloft,' she whispered, 'but it doesn't matter.' She wanted him, it was as simple as that. She wanted him *tonight*.

Lifting the knocker, she brought it down heavily. Then she waited and knocked again but Gideon did not answer.

Briefly she frowned then smiled a bright, tight smile. How silly of her. He was probably taking a shower.

She walked to the back of the house, but the bathroom window was unlighted. Could he be asleep?

She made her way back to the front door and grasped the knocker again.

'Sorry, darling,' she muttered as she brought it down heavily, 'but I'm very determined. I am *not* going home tonight!'

She stood there for an age that lasted all of a minute, but he did not come. She pushed open the letterbox and bending down called, 'Gideon? It's Liri. Wake up, darling!'

She frowned anxiously upward at the tantalizing light then turned the knob only to find the door was securely locked.

For just a second she hesitated, then returned to the assault. Asleep or not, she wouldn't leave until she had had her say. Too much was at stake to give up now.

'I shall stay here till he answers,' she muttered. 'I shall knock and knock till he comes. If he's asleep, then I'll awaken him. Why, if I have to I'll even —' She stopped abruptly, remembering Connie's words. Spoken in jest, of course, but now surprisingly relevant.

'I'll even do that, if I have to!'

'. . . *like heaving a brick through his window,* ' Connie had joked.

'And I will,' Liri resolved. 'I'll make him answer!'

As though her eyes had been directed to the spot she glanced down. A small, smooth cobble lay at her feet, almost as though it had been placed there for a specific purpose.

She picked it up and tossed it into the air. It felt like a cricket ball she thought with pleased surprise, remembering how Gideon had taught her the rudiments of the game.

'You're not bad,' he'd once said grudgingly. 'With a throw like that you'd be good in the outfield – if you were a boy, of course.'

It was a long time since those schoolday cricket matches, but she could still throw a wicked ball, she thought grimly. And now, Gideon would be reminded of how well he had taught her.

She raised her right arm, swinging it into an arc, then held it there questioningly before letting it fall limply to her side. She couldn't do it. Just think of the mess . . . .

She dropped the cobble and scooped up a handful of gravel, then without another thought sent it spattering against Gideon's bedroom window.

It found its target and the noise it made was more than she had bargained for.

'Oh lordy,' she whispered and waited, eyes closed, for the flinging open of the window.

But nothing happened; nothing moved behind the tightly drawn curtains and cupping her hands to her mouth she called, '*Gid*-eon? Sorry, but I –'

But I was desperate. I had to make you answer, she had been going to say, but the words remained unspoken as abruptly the bedroom light snapped off.

'Gideon?' she choked with disbelief.

He had turned out the light so he *must* be awake, she reasoned numbly. He had heard cries – he must have – yet instead of answering her he had reached for the light and deliberately put it out. He had indicated, in the cruellest way possible, that he did not wish to speak to her. The turning-off of that light had been a deliberate snub. It could not have been more hurtful, Liri conceded dismally, if he had answered the door to her knock then slammed it, unspeaking, in her face.

She began to tremble violently, then disbelievingly she turned away.

'Why, Gideon? Why?' she whispered.

Shaking with misery she brushed away a tear. It was so bewildering, so hurtful. It was so hurtful and bewildering, in fact, that there had to be an explanation. Like Gideon had suddenly become deaf, perhaps? Because deaf he must be to have ignored her noise.

She straightened her shoulders and tilted her chin. It wasn't the end of the world; just a small setback. Tomorrow she would try again and it would all come right. Gideon loved her. He *did*.

It was only then that she noticed the car and at first she refused to believe it. How could she have missed it? she frowned. Snugly parked it certainly was, but how could she have been so blind? How could anyone have walked past a bright red sports car?

'Oh, *no*.' Her doubt turned to fear as she remembered Connie's words.

'Who do you know who's got a Spitfire; a little red job?'

She hadn't known then but she did now. The car belonged to Verna Reid who had spent the evening with Gideon and who now was here at Woodsman's Cottage.

That was why Gideon had refused to answer the door. That was why he ignored her knocking. The actress had returned with him and if the evidence was to be believed, was staying the night. Cold with horror, Liri recalled her

frantic knocking; her impassioned appeal through the
open letterbox; the stones she had hurled against the
window.

How embarrassed they must have been. How dreadful
it must all have sounded to two people who probably
wanted nothing more than to be left alone. What had
they thought of her?

Liri closed her eyes and fought the nausea inside her.
What a fool she had made of herself. What an exhibition
she had given. How could she have done such a thing?
Dry-eyed and shocked, she began to run. She ran without
stopping and finally collapsed, breathless, on the chintz-
covered sofa-bed. There was still a faint glow from the
fire and she stared into it, wide-eyed.

'I don't believe it,' she whispered. *'I do not believe it.'*

Her heart began to thump heavily as she remembered
the intimate scene at the inn.

Verna Reid's face was bright with animation and
Gideon had gazed down into her eyes, his arm resting
amicably around her shoulders. They could have been
taken for close, warm friends, each easy in the other's
company, the attraction between them obvious and
mutual.

And now they were together at Woodsman's. It seemed
they were in Gideon's bedroom; they could even be
sharing his bed.

'Say it, you little fool,' she hissed. 'Gideon and Verna
Reid are having an affair. Last night it was me he said he
loved; tonight it's someone else.'

Verna Reid had arrived in Abbeyfield as if by
arrangement and clearly this was not the first time she
and Gideon had met.

What am I to do? she asked silently as her eyes
swivelled of their own accord, almost, to the telephone in
the hall outside.

Connie, she thought, rising to her feet. Connie would

be back in London, now. She would know what to do.

She reached out for the phone and in that instant it began to ring. Startled, she pulled back her hand then, with a cry of relief, she snatched up the receiver. It was Gideon. It had to be.

'Hullo?' she choked.

'Roz! I've been ringing all evening. Where've you been, for goodness sake?'

'James?'

He was doing it again; zooming in on her when her defences were down. He was always doing it, she thought dully.

'Roz? What's the matter?'

'Nothing at all, James.' Her voice sounded clear and cool and totally unconcerned.

'Darling, I'm sorry I was a bit naughty this afternoon. Didn't spoil anything, did I?'

'No, James.' What had there been to spoil? Come to think of it, what had there ever been?

'I mean, I felt some pretty icy vibes from your direction and the worthy Constance seemed very put out, too.'

'You're imagining it.'

'Am I? Well, that's all right, then. I suppose I shouldn't have said what I did, but – well, damn it Roz it's been going on long enough and we've got to talk. You realize that, don't you?'

'I – I suppose so,' she hesitated reluctantly. And maybe it would be as well, she thought. Maybe now they could settle things between them, once and for all.

'When can I see you, Roz? Tomorrow?'

'If you like, James.'

'Of course I'd like – what's got into you? You sound distinctly peculiar. Is someone with you?'

'No. I'm quite alone.'

'Then why don't you come over to Hazlebank Castle? I've an early call for make-up, but I could arrange for a car to pick you up. You'd enjoy it – really you would – and maybe we could get a few minutes together. I can't believe you meant what you said, this afternoon. I really can't believe you meant us —'

'I don't know, James – about coming over, I mean. I've got things to do.' Flower pictures, for instance; more sketches for the rose-hedge design. And what about Gideon? 'Can't it wait?'

'No, I don't think it can. You've kept me dangling far too long. I want something settled between us. In spite of what you said I'd like us to be married as soon as we've finished filming *Night of the Hawkes*.'

'You're rushing me James, and I don't know. I honestly don't know,' she whispered tonelessly. Why had he phoned? And why didn't he hang up? She couldn't cope with his insistence. She had just received a terrible body-blow and right at this moment she couldn't cope with *anything*. 'Phone me later.'

'No, Roz. I'll arrange for a car to pick you up tomorrow. About ten. We can talk, then – all right?'

'All right. Ten o'clock.'

'Good girl. Now go to bed,' he scolded affectionately. 'You sound all-in.'

'I am,' she whispered. 'Goodnight, James.'

She replaced the receiver clumsily, shaking her head in disbelief. It wasn't true; it couldn't be. It wasn't happening to Liri, but to Roz. James didn't know Liri or the secret deeps of Liri's heart.

James would never know Liri's passion, feel her heart beating crazily against his. No man would ever know her intimately, because Liri belonged to Gideon.

But James was welcome to Rosamund Haslington, she thought, staring dully into the mirror. James could have the slab-faced Roz who stared back, dry-eyed. Liri had gone for ever. Tonight, all that was left of her, all that was left of a long-ago love, had wraithed away, sighing.

And better that way, she thought flatly as she walked slowly up the stairs, for Liri belonged to the past; to moon-lit winter nights and toast made at Nanny's fireside. Liri belonged to April and the *liriconfancies* that budded beneath the rose hedge. Liri was bonded to June days and summer-blue skies and warm nights that were heady with the scent of honeysuckle and newly cut hay.

She went to stand by the window, accustoming her eyes to the darkness, staring into the night until she could distinguish the outline of Woodsman's chimneys.

And Liri loved you, Gideon, only now she's taken enough. Liri is opting out in favour of Roz, who is tough. Roz is the one who handed in the keys that night then left Abbeyfield with her head held high. It's only Liri you can hurt, Gideon, and from this moment she is banished. Now it's Rosamund Haslington you'll be seeing from hereto on.

And Roz can live without you.

Nine

When she opened the letter next morning Liri should have felt elated, because even before she read it she knew instinctively that Hathaway-Paige was interested in the sketches she had sent them.

We like your Rose Hedge design, she read, *and feel it might well be extended to include sheets, pillow cases, etc. Perhaps we can meet and talk it over?*

Not so long ago she had hoped desperately for her first Abbeyfield design to do well, yet now, when its success was being obliquely confirmed, she felt nothing at all. Once – yesterday, even – she would have rushed to tell Connie, yet now she was only conscious of a dull misery that gnawed at her like a toothache.

Aimlessly she drew back the living-room curtains, thinking about the previous night, wondering if it had really happened or if she dreamed it.

'It happened,' she said out loud, 'and what's more you made a complete fool of yourself.'

She closed her eyes against the memory of her humiliation then paused at the foot of the stairs to stare without feeling at the message-pad beside the telephone.

Hazlebank. 10 a.m. James. she had written.

Dispassionately she considered the two men; the one who wanted her because she remained aloof; the other who had confirmed his hold over her then shrugged her aside.

Deliberately she forced herself to think about the letter from Hathaway-Paige. Connie would be so glad, but then she always was. Dear Con. A small, sad tear ran down Liri's cheek and she brushed it impatiently away and swallowing hard on a sob of self-pity acknowledged that much as she wanted to hear the voice of a friend it would be pointless to phone. Connie would only ask about Gideon.

'And I couldn't bear it,' she whispered forlornly. 'I couldn't tell her about Verna Reid and that hateful little car outside Woodsman's.' She shook her head impatiently. 'And I'm talking to myself now, but that's what happens when you live alone.'

Yet hadn't she chosen to live alone? In a flush of nostalgia she had returned to Abbeyfield and now she was being forced to face the consequences of her impetuosity.

'But the sooner I leave here, the better,' she whispered. 'The sooner I —'

Leave? Put up a For Sale notice then steal away, exactly as she had done before?

She glared at the bedside clock. It was nearly 9.30 and James was sending a car for her at ten, she reminded herself, glad she could postpone the decision-making for just a little while longer.

And why, she brooded as she turned on the shower, had she agreed to visit the film-set at Hazlewood Castle? Why did James always seem able to zoom in on her when she least wanted him?

And what would she say when he asked her to marry him? Because ask her he *would*.

She wriggled out of her nightdress and flicked it aside with a petulant toe. She ought to say yes, she reflected. James was attentive and attractive. He was becoming successful, too, and could easily afford a wife and children.

But it was Gideon's children she wanted, she argued crossly. She would never stop loving him and no matter what he had done she knew she would forgive him gladly. If he knocked on her door this very minute she would run to him and —

But he wouldn't come. He had spent the night with Verna Reid and if he stood on her doorstep right now she would —

'I'd run to him,' she finished. 'Like the stupid little fool I am, I'd —'

She bit hard on her bottom lip then lifted her face to the softly-warm water. And the water mingled with the tears that ran down her cheeks and washed them away. But still she wept.

At ten o'clock she was waiting, chin on hand, for the car that would take her to Hazlebank Castle. Now she felt calm and cold and drained of emotion. Now she would hand over to Roz, she thought bleakly. Roz would sort out the mess. And why, she thought crossly, had she not insisted on driving there herself?

But James was nobody's fool, she shrugged. He was having her collected because he didn't trust her. James was always one step ahead, she acknowledged dully. With uncanny accuracy he seemed to fix it so that he was never far away – if only in thought.

She heard the car, then, and looked out of the window. And at once she wished she had not, for the car that sped past the top of the lane was small and racy and red, and in it sat two people.

Liri's mouth ran dry with distaste. Where were they going, Verna and Gideon? To London, perhaps, to continue their fling? Or was she taking him to Hazlebank Castle to display like a trophy? Turning sharply away, Liri blanked out her thoughts.

Gideon could no longer hurt her, she insisted. Everything had changed. It changed a long time ago but she was too blind to see it. Maybe she had been wrong to leave Abbeyfield all those years ago but she'd been equally foolish to return. She should have forgotten Gideon and Liri, too; put them both out of her mind and –

The phone began to ring and she hurried to answer it.

'Darling! It's James. Sorry Roz, but we'll have to call it off, this morning. They've wished this publicity thing on us right out of the blue and I don't know when we'll be finished.'

'It's all right.' Relief sang through her. She hadn't wanted to go. She wanted to stay in her safe little house and wrap her unhappiness around her. 'Some other time, maybe?'

'You do understand, Roz? We're doing interviews and shots for a television magazine, but the Press will be there too and we need all the publicity we can get.'

'I know, James. I said it's all right,' she insisted. 'Ring me later?'

'Of course I will, but darling – about what we said last night? If I asked you again to marry me – asked you for the very last time – would you say yes?'

'I – I don't know.'

'Then put it another way. Would you give me a flat, final no?'

'You're hustling me.' Panic tore through her. 'Marriage is too important a thing – it needs a lot of thought.'

What was she saying? Why couldn't she tell him no?

Flatly, finally *no*.

'So you wouldn't turn me down, Roz? I can hope?'

'Yes, James,' she whispered dully, 'you can hope.'

Why was she being so stupid?

'Darling,' he breathed. 'You know how much I want you? I'd make you happy – you know that, don't you?'

'Yes, James. But phone me tonight? 'Bye . . .'

''Bye, my darling. I love you.'

Always the last word, she thought crossly. He gets the better of me every time. I want to tell him no, absolutely *no*. And I'd have had said it, too, if he'd given me the chance!

Carefully she replaced the receiver. It wasn't that she was a coward, she admitted reluctantly. It was just that this morning James had caught her when her defences were down.

Petulantly she trailed into the kitchen and filled the kettle. She didn't love him and miserable as she was she was sure – well, almost sure – that she could never marry him. But he wanted her and right now her wounded pride needed a crutch. She could take no more. Liri – yes, and Roz, too – needed a shoulder to cry on and if that shoulder belonged to James Howard, then was it so very wrong?

Slab-faced she went through the motions of coffee-making, then taking a biscuit from the tin retreated to the saneness of her studio.

'Work,' she muttered, settling herself at the drawing-board, and pushing all other thoughts from her mind, gazed purposefully at the sketches pinned there.

So the manufacturers would like the range extended? she frowned. Palest green pillow-cases scattered with white lily-heads, perhaps? Rose-coloured towels, pink-budded? Sheets with a trellis design of climbing roses?

An artist again, she reached for her sketch-pad. She had work to do and nothing, not even a heart that hurt unbearably, must be allowed to interfere with that work. James would ring again tonight and until then she would forget him she told herself firmly. And she would forget Gideon and —

But already he had ceased to exist. Gideon belonged to Liri and Liri was banished. Tight-lipped, Rosamund Haslington began to work. And she worked until lunchtime and through lunchtime. She heard the church clock strike three and still she sat absorbed, and an hour later the world outside was still a dim and distant place. Then she laid aside her crayon and covered her face with her hands. She was hungry and tired, too, and she had done more than enough for one day.

Slipping from her stool she placed her hands in the small of her back and stretched like a cat. The sketches were good and the pencilled notes beside them made sense. Towels, bed-sheets, wallpaper – all were taking shape. The Rose Hedge design would be a winner, she conceded, yet the realization gave her no joy because now she must come down to earth again and face the problems that still awaited her. Soon she must come to a decision about this little house. Would she ask Mr Butterworth to sell it for her; tell him she was finding that working away from London was not as convenient as she had hoped? Should she wait a little while longer?

It was almost a relief when the phone began to ring. Saved yet again, she thought with relief and picking it up murmured her number.

'Roz! What happened? You said you'd ring.'

'Con. Sorry. I – well, nothing happened. Gideon wasn't there, Con. Colin must've got it wrong.'

'I see. Now tell me the truth.'

'It *is* the truth.' Liri's cheeks flamed. 'I – I was going to phone you later,' she mumbled. 'And such good news, Con. The manufacturers are interested in the Rose Hedge design. They want me to go and see them.'

'Manchester or London, Roz?'

'I don't know. I haven't been in touch with them yet.'

'But why ever not? What's got into you? You should've been on the phone like a shot. Work isn't all that easy to come by, you know.' She stopped and Liri heard the sharp intake of her breath. Then she asked softly, 'You're all right, Roz? You're not sickening for anything?'

'I'm fine, truly I am. As a matter of fact I've been working all day and suddenly I'm hungry. Think I'll grab a quick bite then take a walk. It's been a lovely day here.' She wasn't making sense, but it didn't matter as long as they kept off the subject of Gideon. 'Look, Con, this call's costing the earth. Why don't I ring you back when it's cheaper?'

'All right.' Connie Davies's voice oozed suspicion. 'Be in touch, then?'

'I will. Promise.'

Liri replaced the receiver. What a mess it all was. What a stupid, heartbreaking mess.

Closing her eyes she counted slowly to ten, then picking up the phone again she dialled Hathaway-Paige's number.

Appointment made, Liri wrote *Mr Paige. London. 12.30, Tues.* on the telephone-pad then gazed restlessly around her.

She didn't want to talk to Connie. Not until she had everything straight in her mind would she make the promised call. And right now, her mind was in a terrible muddle.

Best she should go for that walk, she decided, reaching for her coat. She would walk down her lane, look at her fields, try to make sense of it all.

But everything had changed, she reasoned silently as she climbed the paddock stile. Even her lovely old house had been burned into ashes.

But the gardens are still there, the voice of optimism reminded, and breathtakingly beautiful now with the flowers of May. And the last of Queen's Reach land remained; the four acres which now were hers.

'And I love them,' she whispered, 'just as I once loved Queen's Reach.'

It had been one of the reasons for buying Southgate; heart over head and without thought, so an unknown farmer should not have the two small fields. But that farmer was Gideon, she argued, and if she put Southgate on the market, then he could have those fields, and Meadowsweet Lane, too.

And she wanted him to have them, because she still loved him, she admitted dully. And when Queen's Reach was completed she hoped he would love it as she had loved that cold, crumbling house the fire had destroyed.

She stopped and inhaled deeply. The scent in her nostrils was sweet and familiar and evoked memories.

'The lilies. They're out at last,' she whispered, hurrying toward the rose hedge.

Now she could pick some; place them in her workroom, so the design she was working on should be exactly right.

She bent down and the scent was overpowering. It wasn't fair, she yearned. She wanted to do the sensible thing; to cut her losses and make a new start. She needed to forget Abbeyfield and Gideon and the remembered joy of his closeness, yet the rose hedge was in leaf again and the scent of the *liriconfancies* made her ache with longing.

She buried her nose in the cool white flowers then walked purposefully across the stableyard to gaze dispassionately at Northgate Lodge and at the stables, the coach-house and the hayloft, of course. Now they had been arranged into one house and very soon that house would belong to Gideon and there would be a Whitaker at Queen's Reach again.

But would he care as those other Whitakers had cared?

Would he gather in more acres and would his son add more rooms? Tight-lipped she pushed open the front door and taking note of the Wet Paint signs, stepped carefully into the light, bright entrance hall.

Just one last look, she thought, so I can remember it whenever I smell lilies or see a pink rosebud. One last look at what was once a hayloft, so that when my heart remembers my head will tell me that the past has gone for ever.

Slowly she walked up the new staircase, trailing her hand along the graceful sweep of the banister rail, lifting her eyes to the tall window at the bend in the stairs.

It was all so beautiful; smaller than the old Queen's Reach, but a gracious house; one to be lived in and loved in. A house to fill with children. A home.

Reaching the landing she stood for a moment to get her bearings then pushed open the door at the end of the passage to her left. This was the place. This strange new room that once was witness to their love.

She gazed around, willing her heart to be still, then walked over to the west-facing window and lifted her face to the early evening sun.

This will be Gideon's room, she considered, carefully placing the flowers on the window-ledge. The wardrobes to the left will be his and those on the other wall will be hers. And their bed will stand between those wall-lights.

She wished she could find fault with the room, but the fitted furniture in a soft magnolia shade was exactly what she herself would have chosen and she wished she could design the soft-furnishings to complete the room. Something very special. The Rose Hedge design, perhaps?

An icy finger touched the bones of her back. What if by some awful coincidence the unknown woman who would one day sleep here should choose that very fabric? What if rose-hedge towels should find their way into the bathroom and rose-trellis sheets to the bed?

Mentally Liri called a halt. Gideon had hurt her for the

very last time. Maybe she would marry James; maybe she would not, but she was done with the past. She was starting anew and immediately she returned from her visit to Mr Paige, she would put her little house on the market and go back to London where she rightly belonged. She had wished Gideon into her life; had stood at the beech tree and wished for just one glimpse of him and now she must wish him out of it.

It was then she heard footsteps on the stairs and her heart raced wildly as the bedroom door opened.

Stubbornly she stood there, staring over the gardens. She would not turn round. She dare not, because she knew who had entered the room. Even when he spoke her name she still stared ahead, trying to control the shaking inside her.

'Liri.' He said her name again and this time it was a command. Reluctantly she turned to face him.

He was wearing jeans and a checked shirt and had obviously been to collect the evening paper.

Sick inside her she looked into his narrowed eyes then gazed at the toes of her shoes, willing her heart to behave.

You love him still! it exulted, while at the same time her lips formed words for a stranger to speak.

'I came to pick some lilies. I hope you don't mind.'

She nodded toward the flowers and he shrugged and laid his newspaper beside them.

'Be my guest.' He crossed the room to where she stood, then leaned against the wall.

Too close, warned Liri's head and she took a backward step.

'Kicking over the traces, Liri?'

'No. Just taking a last look.' The words came calmly but that was to be understood for now it was Roz who spoke. 'I've decided that Abbeyfield doesn't suit me, you see, and I'm putting Southgate Lodge on the market. So you can have the four acres if you still want them – and

Meadowsweet Lane.'

'I see.' He took a step toward her and this time she did not move away.

'Well?' she choked, when the comment she had expected was not forthcoming. 'Didn't you want that land?'

'You know what I wanted,' he said roughly, grabbing her wrist, holding it tightly so she knew better than to struggle.

'You've a peculiar way of showing it,' she hissed.

'Have I?' Roughly he pulled her closer, then his mouth found hers and because he had anchored her hand behind her back, she found it impossible to move.

Yet she did not want to, because the girl in his arms was Liri, and Liri loved him. She spoke his name huskily and his hand relaxed its hold.

Run! warned Roz, but Liri's lips throbbed with need and she closed her ears to the voice of reason.

'Gideon.' She whispered his name again and her hands slid upward to his neck. Then she cupped his head in her hands drawing him closer, searching with her mouth for his, relaxing against him because suddenly her knees refused to support her.

His lips returned her kiss, but he did not speak. Instead, he loved her with his hands, trailing them over her thighs, her arms; claiming her.

This is the hayloft! Liri's heart rejoiced. Here, it will all come right again.

She pressed closer still, thrilling to his body, and the scent of new-cut hay was back in her nostrils and she wanted him with an urgency so desperate that she cried, 'Gideon! What is happening to us?'

He released her then. He did it with such suddenness it caught her like a slap.

'Darling?' she whispered, but his eyes were inscrutable as ever and she backed away from the scorn in them. 'I –

I tried to tell you. I went to Woodsman's to find you, but
you weren't there.'

'Last night?' he shrugged. 'I had an appointment.'

'Yes. I went to the Coach House, too.' She hadn't
wanted to say it, but her lips formed the words unaided.
'You were there, with Verna Reid.'

'So I was.' He seemed totally unimpressed at the
mention of the actress's name. 'I've known her for some
time. We met in London, ages ago.'

'And?' Liri whispered.

'And I took her out for a meal. Is there any reason why
I shouldn't?'

Bewildered, Liri shook her head. What was happening?
She had tried to meet him half-way and hope had leaped
briefly inside her when their lips met so passionately. Yet
now he was standing aloof again and the coldness was
back in his eyes as if their fleeting encounter had counted
for nothing.

'I was only trying to say —' She stopped as the hostility
in his eyes threw out a warning. 'Oh, well. The company
you keep is no concern of mine I suppose, but I do object
to being made a fool of.'

'Such as?'

'Such as being followed here and your doing what –
well, doing what you did. Surely I don't have to remind
you that this is no longer a hayloft, though you act as if it
is and that I'm still the impressionable girl you once
knew.'

'And you're not, of course.' He looked at her with
something akin to pity. 'Oh, but you've changed, Liri.'

'Don't call me that,' she snapped. 'I'm Rosamund
Haslington now. Liri's gone, Gideon. She left Abbeyfield
almost eight years ago, if you remember?'

'I remember. And fool that I was, I thought she had
come back.'

'No. It's Roz you're talking to now, and Roz doesn't

much care for men who say they love her then storm out
of her life and spend the night with another woman.'

She had said it! She hadn't meant to and she certainly
hadn't wanted to. Indeed, for just a little while it had
seemed that things might come right between them. But
Gideon was playing with her emotions again; taking her
into his arms and establishing his hold over her, then
thrusting her away.

'Well?' she demanded when he refused to answer her
challenge.

'Well, *nothing*,' he hissed, offering not one word of
explanation or regret.

'Oh, surely you're not going to try to deny that Verna
Reid spent the night at Woodsman's?' she flung.

'No. She was there, as you obviously know.'

'Then what in heaven's name are we doing here?' Liri
gasped.

'Doing here? You, I understand, are taking a last look
at what was once a hayloft, and I, if I may be allowed, am
here to offer you my sincere good wishes for your future
happiness.'

He reached for her again, and because she was so
utterly bewildered she made no protest when he folded
her into his arms and kissed her again with savage
intensity. 'I told you once before to enjoy your *James-
darling*. I said I hoped you'd remember me whenever you
were in his arms and that wish still holds good, Liri. So
enjoy your petty little triumph. Like I said, you and he
deserve each other.'

His hands tightened on her arms and his jaw formed
itself into a frightening trap. Then he released her and
the moment of tension was gone.

'W-what are you talking about?' she gasped.

'Talking about? Oh, Liri, come off it. I'm talking about
this!' He reached for the folded newspaper. 'I was on my
way to see you and I saw you crossing the paddock. I

followed you, hoping I suppose, that maybe there'd been some mistake.'

'I don't know what you're talking about!' She was almost weeping with frustration. *'Tell me!'* she demanded harshly.

'Here!' He thrust the paper into her hands. 'Read Seth Hilton's column; you should find it interesting. There's a bit in it about you. Local girl Rosamund Haslington, he calls you!'

'Seth Hilton?' she choked, frowning.

'Yes, and gossip columnist or not, I've usually found him very accurate though I must admit I didn't know about your award. You should have told me, though it only makes me wonder what else you didn't tell me about.' His smile was pure irony. 'But maybe it *is* as you said. Liri's gone,' he shrugged, 'and to be perfectly honest, I couldn't care less what happens to Roz.' He lifted his hand in a gesture of dismissal. 'Goodnight, Miss Haslington. Be happy.' And turning abruptly he closed the door firmly behind him and ran swiftly down the stairs.

Shocked and numb Liri stood with closed eyes, listening to his retreating footsteps. Only then could she bestir herself, staring at the newspaper in her hands, not wanting to open it but knowing she must.

'Seth Hilton?' She unfolded the pages, searching them for the mystical name.

James, warned a voice inside her. It's all to do with James. And she was right, and it was. On page ten she saw his smiling picture. James in tight breeches and a wide-sleeved shirt, open to his waist. James in his *Night of the Hawkes* costume laughing back at her, his eyes mocking.

She drew in her breath, remembering his phonecall. Publicity, hadn't he said? Something for a television magazine, and maybe the Press would be there, too. And amongst them, no doubt, a Seth Hilton who wrote gossip about local affairs.

She had no need to read the whole of his writings because her name leaped out at her unbidden.

. . . on the set of Night of the Hawkes, *parts of which are being filmed on location at Hazlebank Castle, I spoke to James Howard who plays the male lead in Northern Television's eighteenth century epic. Though a southerner born, Mr Howard shows amazing good taste in choosing a wife from one of our northern shires and today announced his engagement to local girl Rosamund Haslington. Miss Haslington, who lives in Abbeyfield, is one of our up-and-coming young artists, having last year won the coveted Newnes Award for textile design.*

The couple hope to visit Abbeyfield from time to time, Mr Howard confided, although their home will of necessity be in London. We wish them a long and happy marriage.

'Oh, *no.*' Liri closed her eyes beseechingly. James had done it again and this time he had excelled himself. For once, *just for once*, she had not given him a flat refusal and he had taken it to mean that she had given in at last.

But did it matter? James had succeeded where eight years of separation had failed and nothing could matter now, save that she should get out of this room and the memories it evoked. Without thinking she reached for the lilies, then clutching them tightly she began to run. Nor did she stop until breathless she reached her little house.

She heard the ringing of the telephone as she reached her door and was almost tempted to stand there outside until it stopped. But she answered it because she knew instinctively who it would be.

'I thought you'd ring, James,' she whispered, her breathing still uneven.

'Are you all right, Roz?'

'Give me one good reason why I shouldn't be?'

'I was wondering if you'd seen the evening paper?'

He sounded uncertain, Liri thought with amazement. For once, James Howard seemed apprehensive and unsure.

'I saw it,' she retorted, flatly.

'And you'll forgive me – for jumping the gun, I mean? If I hadn't done it that way you'd never have said yes, Roz. All I ask is that you give me a chance to explain?'

'All right James, though I won't say it didn't come as a shock. After all, it isn't every day a girl learns from a – a gossip column that she's just got herself engaged.'

'Listen, darling – I've finished for the day; give me half an hour to get my make-up off and then I'll be over to see you. Let's talk it over.'

'Sorry, but I really am busy. I've got phonecalls to make and I want to get my portfolio together. I'm going to London first thing tomorrow and to be quite truthful, I don't particularly want to see anyone right now.'

'All right, Roz. But promise me not to do anything rash, like denying it out of hand? I *can* make you happy; all I want is the chance. Don't think too badly of me.'

'I won't. You shouldn't have done what you did, but I *will* think about it, James.'

'And you'll remember that I want you very much?'

'I'll remember. And I'll ring you when I get back.'

Unnaturally calm, she replaced the receiver. Strange, she thought, it had been almost as though she were standing there listening as some other woman made the call. Liri listening to Roz.

Sighing softly she dialled the number of Connie's shop. Best get it over with.

'What's going on, Roz?' her friend demanded. 'Have you seen the early evening editions?'

'I have,' Liri replied coolly. 'We have them here, too.'

'Then *why*, for Pete's sake? Just what do you think you're doing?'

'It's all such a mess . . . .'

'Never mind the mess – is it *true?*'

'Well – er – yes, and no.'

'And what kind of an answer is that?'

'I don't know. I can only say for certain that it was a surprise to me, too.'

'And to Gideon Whitaker, I shouldn't wonder.'

'Don't, Con.' Liri had had enough. 'I'll tell you about it tomorrow. I'm seeing Mr Paige in the London office, and I'll stay the night with you if that's all right?'

'You know it is. Stay as long as you like.'

As long as she liked, Liri sighed as she replaced the receiver. Why, come to think of it, had she ever left?

But slowly things were sorting themselves out. Now, for the first time, she knew exactly what she must do, and picking up the telephone again dialled another number. And when it answered she spoke firmly and clearly as only Roz could be relied upon to do.

'Good afternoon. I'd like to speak to Mr Butterworth, if he's there. Tell him it's Miss Haslington from Abbeyfield, will you . . . ?'

Ten

Liri sat in the big leather armchair, feet pulled beneath her, staring into the fire. It was good, she thought, to be back in the flat once more; to be sheltered by Connie's saneness from the traumas and tragedies of the past few weeks.

Reluctantly she pulled her gaze from the hypnotic flickering of the fireglow to murmur, 'I had a good afternoon with Mr Paige. He wants to open up the range, really go to town on the Rose Hedge design. I'll be busy for quite some time.'

'Good. I'm pleased for you.' Connie lifted the coffee pot, raising a questioning eyebrow, but Liri shook her head.

'No thanks. Another cup would only keep me awake.'

'Hm. I see what you mean. You look as if you could do with an early night – or perhaps it isn't any of my business?'

'Or in other words, what's been happening?' Liri supplied.

'Now that you mention it – yes. Well, I've been busy since the weekend – sketches and things; getting a portfolio together for Mr Paige –'

'OK. And Mr Paige was impressed. That was the good news; now let's have the bad. And don't look so indignant, lovey. It's your old mate you're talking to now; Constance, the keeper of your conscience, remember?'

'Oh, all right.' Sighing, Liri closed her eyes. No use trying to deceive Con and anyway, she needed to talk. 'I suppose you've got to know, sooner or later. I've put Southgate on the market.'

'*Selling* it?'

'That's the general idea. Furnished, of course.'

'And when did you dream that one up?'

'It's no dream, Con. It's fact. I phoned Mr Butterworth late yesterday.'

'But *why*, for heaven's sake?'

'Oh – *because* . . . .'

'Because you've suddenly decided you're a Londoner, after all? I find that a bit hard to believe – especially after seeing your lovely Abbeyfield.'

'No. I like it here in London, but Abbeyfield will always be home.'

'Then what's got into you? I expected to hear from you on Sunday night, but never a word. Then all I get is prevarications and still I'm in the dark. But it's all to do with Gideon Whitaker. *He's* at the bottom of all this, isn't he?'

'If you mean am I going to marry him then no, I'm not.'

'I see. And am I to be told why?'

'Do you really want to know?' Liri gasped. 'Do you want all the sordid details? Would it please you to know that when I got to Woodsman's that night, Gideon had left? And when I eventually found him, would you believe me if I said he was drinking champagne with Verna Reid?'

'The actress, you mean? The one James brought with

him to Southgate?'

'That's her. And since we're really rubbing my face in it, the one he spent Sunday night with.'

'Spent the night – you're sure?'

'Quite sure,' Liri retorted crisply. 'She left her car outside, so the evidence was plain to see.'

'Now hold on a bit.' Connie held up a cautionary finger. 'The evidence, as you call it, could have been kind of – er – circumstantial, if you see what I mean?'

'Yes, I'll grant you that,' Liri whispered. 'But I mentioned it to Gideon when next we met – kind of casually, of course and he said no, he wouldn't deny it. She *had* spent the night there. He admitted it.'

'Then if he made a full and free confession, I suppose –' Connie shrugged and sighed. 'Pity, really. Just as I'd made up my mind to come and live there myself.'

'You, Con?' Liri sat bolt upright. 'Live in Abbeyfield?'

'No law against it, is there? Nothing to say I can't marry and settle down there. Or is it —'

'*Marry*, you said? But *who?*'

Liri's cheeks flushed bright pink with shock. Connie getting *married?*

'Well – er — ' Connie regarded the fingernails of her left hand with studied nonchalance. 'Well, if you must know, I'm considering marrying Colin McLeod.'

'B-but I saw him only this morning,' Liri choked. 'He was walking up Meadowsweet Lane to collect the herd for milking. He asked me where I was away to, so early in the morning and I said I was going to London on business then staying the night with you.' She stopped, breathless and unbelieving. 'He didn't say a word,' she finished lamely.

'Well no, he wouldn't.' The fingernail gaze did not waver. 'He doesn't know about it – *yet*. But we'll be married, Roz, even if I have to pop the question myself,' she added calmly.

'Con. You *wouldn't* . . . .'

'Wouldn't I just.' Connie looked up, smiling complacently. 'This is the day of equal opportunities, isn't it? And anyway, it's Leap Year, or had you forgotten?'

'You mean it, don't you?' Liri whispered. 'You really like him? And that was the career girl who was going to give up bread, if I remember rightly.'

'So I was, lovey. But I've developed a strange fondness for it again. All of a sudden I'm partial to the nice Scottish variety – oh, you know what I mean, Roz? Surely you've tasted it? All crisp and crusty on the outside but soft and nice inside?'

'Oh, Con.' It was more than Liri could bear and she covered her face with her hands. 'It's not fair!'

'Hey come on, now. I was only kidding – well, kind of kidding, I suppose. But I *do* like him, Roz and I think he quite likes me, too.'

'I'm sorry. I'm acting like a selfish child. I suppose it was just the thought of you living up there and me being here that got me upset. And you know I'd be the first one to dance at your wedding don't you – no matter who it was you married?'

'I know, Roz. And wish me luck, uh? It might just happen – you never know. Keep your fingers crossed for me. But tell me why, when you were so certain of your feelings for Gideon Whitaker, he suddenly takes up with the Reid woman? Was it because of the engagement announcement? And how did Master James manage to get away with that, might I ask?'

'It's a long and complicated story.' Wearily Liri shook her head. 'It's just one long chapter of errors, starting with the one James made last Sunday afternoon, I suppose.'

'I'll grant him that – his timing is perfect, on or off the stage.'

'I know. It's uncanny,' Liri frowned. 'I can never be free

of him. He seems to appear suddenly or to ring, and almost always when he shouldn't. Sometimes I think I'll just give in.'

'I thought you already had. When I read what was in last night's paper –'

'You can't believe everything you read,' Liri interrupted crossly. 'James had this photo-call, you see – something to do with publicity for *Night of the Hawkes*. It seemed pretty harmless when he told me about it, but I should have known better.'

'But you put it right? You told him it wasn't on?'

'No. It didn't turn out like that at all. The first I knew about it was when Gideon showed it to me, and it wasn't pleasant, I can tell you. I tried to explain, but he didn't want to know. But I suppose I've got to face facts. Gideon's no longer interested. Eight years is a long time.' Her lips began to tremble and she drew in a deep, calming breath. 'All that time I thought I was in love with him – all that wasted time.'

'Maybe so, but we were talking about James and what you should do. Surely you're not going to let him get away with it? It was no more than trickery, and blatant trickery at that. Surely you intend telling him once and for all —'

'I ought to, I know, but I haven't. He said he was sorry for doing what he did, but he still wants to marry me, Con. He's asked me for the last time, he says.'

'So say no, for the last time?'

'It isn't that easy,' Liri whispered. 'I'm not sure. James is attractive and attentive and there must be hundreds of women in love with him.'

'But you're *not*,' Connie supplied flatly. 'Yet suddenly you're considering settling for half a loaf . . . .'

'No, I'm not – not really. I haven't said yes, but I haven't said no, either. And for goodness sake, what's so extraordinary about wanting to be married? I'm alone in the world, Con – what's so wrong in wanting children of my own?'

'Just about everything when you're not in love with the man in question. And when you're as desperately in love as you are with someone else, then having children with James would be downright immoral, to my way of thinking.'

Liri closed her eyes and tried to imagine the first night of a honeymoon spent with James but she saw only starlight through roof tiles and the scent of hay and honeysuckle mocked her senses again.

'I know, Con. I know.' Desperately she shut out the past. 'But try to understand! James wants me and I need to be wanted.'

'So you're prepared to marry him on the rebound?'

'Yes! No! Oh, I'm not sure. If only I knew what to do,' she sighed.

It was exactly then that the phone began to ring and for a second it took Liri by surprise. Then she began to laugh mirthlessly. He was doing it again; beaming-in on her thoughts. What was she to do? she had asked and suddenly James was there at the other end of the telephone; waiting for his answer, willing her to say yes.

'Didn't I tell you?' she gasped. 'He's doing it again. I just can't win, Con.' She rose to her feet. 'Mind if I take it in the bedroom?'

'Yes I do. It's my phone and *I'll* answer it,' Connie administered a sharp push and surprised, Liri sat down again. 'If it's for you, I'll tell you so,' she added, firmly closing the door between them.

'Well, *really!*' Indignantly Liri rose to her feet again as the ringing stopped and holding her breath she tried to hear what was being said on the other side of the partition wall. But it was only a low, monosyllabic murmur and when Connie eventually entered the room again there was nothing in her expression to indicate what had taken place.

'Well?' Liri demanded. 'Was it for me, or wasn't it?'

'It was for you,'

'Then why didn't you call me? Really Con, I —'

'I didn't call you because he didn't ask to speak to you. All he said was for you to meet him tomorrow night at half-past seven.'

'Meet me? But where?'

'I don't know, lovey. I presume that he presumed you'd know.'

'Well, I *don't* know, though I suppose he means Abbeyfield. Doesn't he realize I'm in London?'

'One would think so, considering he's just called you on a London number.'

'Oh, you know what I mean, Con. And didn't I say he was always doing it? I've only to ask what I should do and there he is, like he's got me bugged, or something. And anyway, how did he know I'd be back tomorrow? As – as a matter of fact, I'd thought of staying another day,' she added defiantly.

'I wouldn't do that, if I were you,' came the quiet retort. 'You see, he didn't exactly *ask* you to meet him. It came over more like a command. 'Tell Liri to meet me at half-past —'

'Liri? He said *tell Liri?* James wouldn't say that. He always calls me Roz.'

'So he does, dear – but did I say it was James who rang?'

'*Gideon?*' Liri gasped. 'But it couldn't be; he didn't know I was here. And why is he ringing? And come to that, how dare he order me to meet him?'

'To answer your questions strictly in numerical order, I assure you it was Gideon Whitaker and since you told Colin where you were going, it's a simple matter to find you here.'

'But the number's ex-directory.'

'Ah, well – yes. I gave it to Colin. You never know, I thought. And I was right. And as for why Gideon Whitaker wants to meet you, well, your guess is as good as mine. But I'd say it was probably something to do with Southgate Lodge and its four desirable acres – not to mention Meadowsweet Lane, of course.'

'Y-yes. I suppose you're right,' Liri whispered, elation gone. 'You usually are, Con. It'll only be the land he wants to talk about. It couldn't be about anything else, could it? But why talk to me? Shouldn't he be dealing with the estate agent?'

'I really don't know.' Connie's smile was enigmatic, 'but if you were to ask me I'd strongly advise you to do as he says. He seemed very definite about it.'

'Well, I – I'll think about it,' Liri hesitated. 'After all, he can't expect me to come running the minute he crooks his finger in my direction, can he?'

'Can't he?' Connie laughed out loud. 'But he's just done it, Roz, and what's more you'll go. I'd take bets on it.'

'And you'd probably make a handsome profit, Miss Davies,' Liri whispered into the darkness later that night. 'Because I *shall* go, even though it's only business. I'll go, because where Gideon is concerned I have no pride left. I care, still. I always will, even though at this very moment I'm considering saying yes to James.'

But Connie was right, she frowned. To marry James, to sleep in his arms when she was in love with someone else would be very wrong. And totally unbearable, she added miserably.

'But I want children,' she whispered, yet all the time knowing that only Gideon's children could fulfil that longing. Sons to care for Queen's Reach; daughters to spoil.

We would have beautiful daughters and tall, handsome

sons, she considered, and each of them a love-child.

'Oh, damn!' Angrily she punched the pillow. Would she never get to sleep? Was she to lie awake all night, agonizing over what might have been when all the time the answer was as plain to see as the nose on her face? For years the memory of Gideon had haunted her, making it impossible for any other man to completely own her heart. Yet his love for her had not been so steadfast, it seemed, and it was easy to see that he no longer loved her.

On the other hand, she reflected, there was James who wanted her and was becoming increasingly impatient, yet as she had just acknowledged, marriage without love had no place in her future plans.

So you will tell James it's no use, she silently asserted, and then you will tell Gideon that as far as you are concerned he can go to Canada or anywhere else that takes his fickle fancy.

And then she would sell Southgate Lodge and all its futile dreams and get on with the business of living, again. She would see James as soon as she got back to Abbeyfield. Best she should get it over with as quickly as possible, she stressed, for it wouldn't be easy. She liked him a lot, still – But as a friend, she cautioned silently. Not as the sun and the moon and the beginning and the end. Not as you love Gideon.

'As you *loved* Gideon,' she whispered fiercely. 'It's over and done with. You'll see him tomorrow night; tell him he can have the fields, and then you'll forget him!'

She sighed, turned on to her back, then gazing into the half-light listened to the night sounds, to the hum of London at midnight.

It will be very still, in Abbeyfield, she pondered. Just the cry of a night-bird, maybe, and the murmur of the river. And tomorrow I will be back there to tell Gideon he can have my little house and my fields. And when it's all over I shall lock the door and drive away and I'll never,

ever think of it again. I swear I won't!

Yet when she awoke next morning it was to think of Abbeyfield and Gideon whom she was meeting at half-past seven.

But where? she fretted. Did he think she was a mind-reader? Should she wait at Southgate for his knock, or should she take the field-path to Woodsman's?

Or maybe she would find him leaning on the gate at the end of Meadowsweet Lane, gazing covetously at the four ares, deciding exactly when he would instruct Colin to cut the hay-crop?

Then she closed her eyes miserably for it would be none of those places – she knew it without the shadow of a doubt – for if she herself had said 'Meet me', to Gideon there could only have been one place.

And that was where he would be, she thought tremulously. He intended her to meet him at the Rose Hedge as he had done all those years ago, only this time perhaps he would afford her the courtesy of a goodbye. When he'd got her promise to sell him her fields, that would be.

Yet in spite of her unhappiness she ate the breakfast Connie placed in front of her and accepted a packet of sandwiches for lunch on the train.

'What time will you be back there?' Connie demanded.

'Oh, about half-past two,' Liri murmured absently. 'I'll ring you tonight!'

'Promise? No matter what happens?'

'Now what on earth do you expect to happen?' Liri demanded.

'I don't know but I've got a feeling about it that's all.'

'Then you needn't have,' Liri smiled. 'I know exactly what I'm doing.'

'That's what I'm afraid of.' Connie closed her eyes as an expression of suffering crossed her face. 'Because recently you've used that phrase on more than one occasion, and just look at what's happened.'

'Well it won't happen again,' Liri whispered softly. 'I've learned my lesson.'

'But you'll not do anything silly – if you know what I mean?' Connie's eyes were unusually anxious.

'Regarding James, you mean?'

'James or – or *anyone*.'

'I won't, Con. I've thought it all out. I promise you I'll count to ten before I say anything – to *anybody*.'

'That's all right, then. Shall I come up this weekend, or would you rather be alone?'

'Do you want to?'

'Yes I do. Idiot that I am, I want to very much.'

'Oh Con, I'm a selfish little beast, aren't I? Here's you, longing to come to Abbeyfield and here's me, doing my best to get away from the place. I've made a mess of things, haven't I?'

'Haven't we both?' Connie grinned ruefully. 'And to think I'd ever have got interested in sandy-haired Scotsmen and —'

'Calves called Hamish?' Liri suggested.

'And calves called Hamish,' Connie admitted, pink-cheeked.

'So see you on Friday?' Liri smiled.

'See you. And – well – be careful, uh?'

'I'll be careful,' Liri acknowledged gravely. For she was fully determined to be so. Now that it was all straight in her mind she would not allow herself to be side-tracked.

See James, then meet Gideon, she pondered as the train swayed northward. Tell him he can have Southgate and the fields and Meadowsweet Lane. Smile and wish him well and walk away with your head held high, Liri Haslington. You did it before; you can do it again – and with dignity, this time.

She closed her eyes and bit deeply on her lip. She was glad she was sitting in a crowded compartment of the

King's Cross to York train, because had she been alone, had she now been at Southgate, or walking over her fields, or any place other than this, she would have broken down and cried. She would have cried and cried until there were no tears left.

But I'll cry tonight, she whispered inside her. Tonight, when it's finally over, I'll cry for Liri. And then I'll say goodbye to that soft-hearted kid and Roz will pick up the pieces and get on with the business of living, so help me. And neither of us will fall in love again. Not ever!

On arrival at Southgate Lodge, the first thing Liri did was to ring the number James had given her, and they told her that James had finished filming for the day and suggested she might find him at the White Hart.

'Good,' she sighed, turning on the shower. 'The sooner it's over the better.'

But the meeting with James wouldn't be the end of it, she thought apprehensively, because much as she dreaded having to tell him, there was still worse to follow. Tonight, for instance, at half-past seven. If Gideon came, that was. He did, after all, have a history of broken dates behind him, she frowned.

But he *must* come, she argued silently. She wanted so desperately to see him again, even though she was certain that nothing would come of their meeting but heartache. And he'd be there, she thought grimly. Gideon wanted Southgate and the fields.

She rubbed soap over her arms and abdomen and thought with dismay of the loneliness ahead of her.

I want so much to love and be loved, she yearned. Why can't I say yes to James and try, *really try* to love him?

But it was impossible even to consider it, because once she had loved Gideon. He had been her first love, a sweet-as-summer-honey love and impossible to forget.

184

And he would be her last love, too, she thought sadly because never, not even if she lived to be as old as time, could she forget him.

She shrugged into a robe then reflectively began to towel-dry her hair. Suddenly and strangely she felt more calm, now. She hoped James would be reasonable; she wanted them to stay friends, she pondered as she took slacks and a crisp cotton blouse from the wardrobe.

The afternoon was unusually warm for May and Liri tried to close her eyes and heart to the beauty around her as she drove slowly along the lanes to Hazlebank.

Is the apple blossom always so pink and thick and are bluebells so utterly blue? she wondered, or is Abbeyfield cheating again, trying to make me stay?

With the eye of an artist she looked at the frothy white cow parsley and in the meadows around the clear gold haze of the first buttercups.

Against her better judgment she stopped the car and wound down the window, fixing it all in her mind. In the distance a cuckoo called and it reminded her of another of Gran's sayings and how essential it was to make a wish at the sound of the first cuckoo-call of spring.

'It'll come true, sure as eggs is eggs,' Gran insisted. So foolishly Liri wished. She closed her eyes and crossed her fingers and tremulously wished away the years to a summer night and a girl who waited beside a hedge of roses. She knew it could never be granted, of course. Those sweet years were long-gone and Gideon too, or so she had thought. Yet Gran's superstitions had a grain of truth in them, she reluctantly acknowledged, recalling the bread-and-salt wish she thought had been wasted.

And tonight she would meet Gideon again and it would be the hardest thing she had ever done. After tonight, she realized, nothing that might happen in the future could hurt her as much. After tonight her life would never be the same, because even though they would never

meet again she would always think about him; always
long to meet him once more at the turning of a corner or
at the lifting of her eyes at some crowded, boring party.
The memory of tonight would rule and direct her life for
another eight years. She would never be free of him.

'Stop it!' she hissed. She was going to see James and
tell him finally that she could not marry him, and even
though she was aware of the loneliness she would be
bringing upon herself, she knew she had no choice but to
say it.

She found him eventually in the residents' lounge,
engrossed in a newspaper, and when he saw her he looked
up with unconcealed pleasure.

'Roz! How very nice!' He said it throatily as if he had
been waiting impatiently for hours; as if she were the
most beautiful, the most desirable woman in the world. 'I
didn't expect you until this evening. What a lovely
surprise.' He rose gracefully to his feet and gathered her
tenderly into his arms, tilting her chin with his forefinger
then kissing her mouth warmly. 'How was London?'

'Noisy,' she smiled, 'and rather warm. But I only flew
down on business. The manufacturers are taking up my
designs so I'm going to be rather busy.'

She took a deep, calming breath. Why was she babbling
on so? Why suddenly had she started to shake?

James smiled again then led her to the settee. 'Sit
down, my dear. It's just about time for tea. Let me ring
for a tray?'

'No, James! Er – no thanks. I – I haven't come to talk
pleasantries. I've —'

'Of course you haven't.' He cupped her chin in his hand
and turned her face to his. 'But perhaps we could talk
better in my room?' His eyes slid eloquently to the door,
indicating that what was to pass between them was best

not enacted in a public room.

'No!' She jerked her head free and ran her hands laboriously over the creases in her trousers. 'I – I'd best say it quickly, because it isn't altogether pleasant and I don't relish saying it, but I can't marry you, James. I've thought and thought about it, but I can't.'

At last it was out in the open. Perhaps not in the way she had intended, but at least she had said it.

Wide-eyed she gazed at him, then nervously she rose to her feet and walked over to the window.

'I like you James, and it's been fun,' she whispered, staring out across the garden, 'but I can't see us being married till death us do part and I can't –'

She jumped at the unexpected pressure of his hands on her shoulders then stiffened her body in defence against him.

'James. I – I can't —'

'Sssh, darling.' His lips brushed the nape of her neck. 'You don't know what you're saying.'

She could feel his breath on her ear and she flung round to face him.

'But I do James. I do. And I like you a lot but liking's not enough. You *must* believe me. Our engagement is over – if it ever began, that is.'

'It began for me a long time ago,' he whispered, taking a step toward her, gathering her to him again. 'The first time I saw you, I loved you. You stood there so alone and innocent-looking that I knew I had to protect you and care for you. In that big noisy room I only saw you, my lovely love.'

'B-but it wasn't —'

He silenced her words with his kiss but her thoughts raced on. The room hadn't been big or noisy, she insisted silently. There were only the two of them there, in fact, and Betta Lancaster.

They had been in Miss Lancaster's dressing-room after

a performance of *King Lear*, she remembered. She had never met James before that night; she probably would never have met him had she not been delivering sketches for the actress's approval.

In those early days she was desperate for work, and when Betta Lancaster had mentioned – in Connie's shop, actually – that she would like a drawing of her dog to carry with her each night to the theatre, Connie had secured the commission for her. That was how and where she and James met; not in a crowded, noisy room.

'James, you've got to listen!' She pushed him from her, searching with her eyes for his. 'This isn't a sudden decision. We've never been right together. You've swamped me, stifled me. I've enjoyed being with you, I'll admit it, but you're too *flamboyant* for me. I find the glitter of your life too frightening. I'm a country mouse at heart and —'

And I don't love you. Why couldn't she say it?

'No, Roz. To me you are beautiful. There's a serenity about you that I find irresistible.' His eyes narrowed and for the first time he allowed his feelings to show through. 'But you've changed since you came up here to live and you never fully explained why you did it. Is there someone else?' His hands tightened on her arms. 'Are you cheating on me?'

'I don't think I am, James.' She forced her gaze to remain steady. 'There's nothing to cheat on. We weren't committed.'

'Weren't we? You surprise me. I'd always thought we had an understanding, my dear. That's why I told the Press we were engaged. I thought it was about time someone took the initiative and brought it into the open.'

'James! Why won't you listen? I'm asking you to forget it. Engagements are for two people who like each other and I'm not in love with you, James.'

'So there *is* someone else? There's got to be,' he said

flatly, reaching for her again. 'If you tell me that, my darling, then I'll let you go.' He drew her gently to him and laid his cheek on her hair. 'Tell me? I've a right to know.'

'Yes you have,' she choked. 'Perhaps I should have told you sooner, but I thought he didn't matter any more.'

'And he does?'

'I'm afraid so, James. It happened a very long time ago and I know now there'll never be anyone else.'

'It's that farmer fellow, isn't it? He wants to marry you?'

'It *was*. And he doesn't – want to marry me, I mean. But *I* want *him*. I've no pride left where he's concerned, and if I can't have him —' She shrugged, unable to go on.

'So it's got to be goodbye?' he whispered, his voice tender again. 'I can't believe it, my darling. I can't believe that tomorrow I'll awaken to the certain knowledge that I might never see you again; never hold you —'

'Don't? Please don't make me feel so guilty. It's better this way. It *is*.'

She looked up at him, but he was gazing ahead, his eyes focused on a picture on the wall opposite. As though he were delivering a speech, she thought; speaking above the heads of the audience as actors did, to some distant and inanimate object.

'If it's what you want, then who am I to stand in the way of your happiness? I love you too much for that, my darling girl.'

Liri closed her eyes and almost in resignation rested her head against him once more. Better not to speak. Best let him have his say. He could talk it all out of himself. He was good at words.

Words? Familiar words, almost? He had said them before, she was sure of it.

'But I shall be waiting, if you need me. Just call and I'll

come. Whisper to me, and I'll be there.' His voice was husky with concern as he placed a forefinger beneath her chin and directed her gaze to his. He did it so well, she thought, but she had heard it many times before as she sat among a sighing audience, watching him perform a love-scene to perfection.

And that was what he was doing now; performing lines from a play. She should have recognized them sooner. *Goodbye Tomorrow,* his first West End success. She had seen it four times.

And soon, she thought wildly, he'll take my left hand as he did in the play and he'll kiss each fingertip. And then he'll say, 'Remember that, my yesterday-sweetheart . . . .'

'James,' she choked. 'I beg you – don't say any more.'

But he only smiled, and lifted her left hand, and placing a kiss in its upturned palm he murmured. 'Remember that, my yesterday-sweetheart. Never forget that I shall always be waiting.'

Tenderly he smiled; tenderly he took each finger in turn and kissed them with lips that trembled.

'James – *please.*' There was so much she needed to say; words of regret, of compassion, even. But *real* words, she insisted silently, not tinselled platitudes from a work of fiction. 'I – I must go. I really must.' Her voice shook; not with sadness or pity but with sheer disbelief. 'And I *will* call you if ever I need you. You'll always be my dearest friend.' Damn it ! Now she was acting. 'Goodbye, James.'

'Goodbye, my love.' He held her hand, releasing it slowly and reluctantly in one last theatrical gesture as she backed away. 'Goodbye, dear heart . . . .'

I shall scream, Liri thought as she closed the door behind her. Either that or I'll laugh and laugh till I burst. I can't believe it. I *can't!*

But she had heard it with her own ears she insisted as she ran to her car. James had realized he'd failed and had retreated defensively into make-believe because that was the only place in which he was truly in command. He didn't love her; he couldn't have taken her rejection so calmly if he had. She had convinced him finally of the futility of their relationship and he had turned her rebuttal into a performance.

'Oh, James!' She slammed the car door then collapsed over the car wheel in mirthless laughter. 'Always the actor; right up to the last gasp!'

She laughed soundlessly until a tear ran down her cheek and was brushed impatiently away. Then she took a slow, sobering breath.

That's it then, Liri, she thought dismally. You expected anger and drama – passion, even. You thought he'd persuade and protest but all he did was to give you a polished performance from the last act of one of his stage successes. He didn't love you. He wanted you only because he couldn't have you and when he realized it was over, he cut his losses and delivered an eloquent face-saver. And that's all you meant to him, my girl. He was probably doing a run-through of more available females even as he spoke.

Carefully she eased the car on to the road.

'So you're on your own again, Roz Haslington,' she whispered flatly. After tonight, that was, when she and Gideon met; when she gave back her acres to Queen's Reach where they belonged. Tonight, when hopefully they would say goodbye like civilized people.

Then I'll walk away with my head held high, she silently vowed. I'll do it if it kills me!

Tonight. Unhappy, unwanted tonight at the rose hedge.

Only this time she was eight years wiser and this time it was Roz who would wait there. And Roz would not weep.

Eleven

Liri was filling the kettle when the bright red sports car drove up the lane.

'Well! Of all the *cheek*,' she gasped, wondering whether or not to answer the impatient knocking. But curiosity triumphed and she opened the door.

'Good evening.' A flush of annoyance reddened her cheeks. 'I'm afraid I'm on the point of going out, Miss Reid.'

'What I've come to say won't take long,' came the equally brusque retort. 'Might I come in?'

Reluctantly Liri led the way into the sitting-room. 'I have an appointment at half-past seven,' she warned.

'Don't worry. I won't keep you.' Elegantly the actress lowered herself into the armchair and crossing her legs to advantage, rested a graceful hand on each chair-arm.

She's like James, Liri thought incredulously. They do everything so *beautifully*.

'I want to talk to you about James,' Verna said without

preamble. 'I understand that your engagement is off?'

'It was never actually on,' Liri countered bluntly. 'But I don't see —'

'What it's got to do with me? But my dear good girl, it's got everything to do with me. That's why I need to know if what James has just told me is really true.'

'It's true,' Liri admitted.

'Good. Then we know where we stand. James appears to be taking it remarkably well, but I wouldn't like to think it might flare up again, as it were?'

'Now look here —'

'No, Miss Haslington, *you* look. I've watched your so-called romance for two years, almost, and if you'd cared for James as I care for him, you'd have been wedded and bedded long before now. So let's not be coy, ducky! And what about Gideon Whitaker? Where does he fit in?'

'Gideon? You sit there, calm as you please and ask about Gideon when you know better than I do where he fits in! You should do, considering you spent *all* of Sunday with him. And don't deny it, because I saw your car. I was there, you see.'

'Yes. I heard you.' Verna smiled acidly. 'And the mood you were in made me decide against opening the door. But aren't you jumping to entirely the wrong conclusions?'

'You think so, when you've admitted it and Gideon admitted it, too.'

'Did he?'

'He most certainly did,' Liri countered hotly. 'I asked him outright if you'd spent the night at Woodsman's and he said you had.'

'Then what a pity you didn't ask him where *he* slept that night. Because if you had, he'd have told you he spent the night at the farm.'

'K-Keeper's Lodge?' Liri gasped, suddenly deflated.

'If that's Colin McLeod's place – yes.'

'You mean I got it wrong?' Liri whispered.

'Very wrong. And far from spending a night of wining and dining and abandoned love, I'm afraid the whole night-out was something of a catastrophe. Apart from spending the better part of the evening extolling your virtues, my host also drank rather too much and I had to drive him home – in *my* car. Then I found I'd got a flat tyre and the gallant Gideon said he'd fix it for me – but in daylight, if I didn't mind.' She paused dramatically, eyebrow raised. 'Then he threw me his house-keys, told me I'd find clean sheets in the airing cupboard, and announced that he was going to Colin's place.'

'And then what?' Liri murmured.

'Then nothing. Next morning Master Gideon had recovered sufficiently to change my wheel and I drove him to the Coach House to pick up his own car. Like I said, not my idea of a night out, but it was my own fault for taking pity on him when he rang, I suppose. I was a little put out myself, at the time.'

'So you – you *didn't* . . .?' Liri held her hands to her blazing cheeks.

'We did *not,* I assure you. So in return for that priceless piece of information, I reckon you should play fair with me and keep away from James until I've convinced him that it's me he loves. All right.'

'I have no intention of getting in touch with James again,' Liri gasped, 'and might I say that I think you're very forthright, Miss Reid?'

'You may and I am. We live in that kind of world, unfortunately. And for goodness sake call me Verna,' she flung, irritably.

For a few seconds they gazed warily at each other, then smiling reluctantly, Liri held out her hand.

'And I'm Liri – although it's really Roz – well, Rosamund, actually.'

'So we understand each other, Liri?'

'We do indeed, Verna.'

'Fine. Then I'll be on my way.' The actress rose to her feet, then glancing at the sideboard and the unopened bottle of elderflower wine, she murmured, 'Is that stuff *really* potent? I mean, can it actually do what Miss Davies threatened?'

'Depending on the mood of the drinker – that, and more. But why don't you try it out? Be my guest,' Liri smiled, offering the bottle.

'Well, thanks.' Verna Reid regarded it gravely. 'Wish me luck, then?'

'I do,' Liri murmured solemnly. 'I wish you all the luck in the world. And thanks. Thanks a lot.'

She stood bemused at the window and watched her new-found ally drive away. 'Well, fancy that,' she murmured incredulously. 'And right out of the blue . . . .'

But why Gideon had let her jump to the wrong conclusions when one small word of denial would have been sufficient?

But it was *your* fault, she silently admonished the bright-eyed mirror picture. You can't blame him for not denying an accusation like that. It was quite unthinkable and totally undeserving of a reply.

And now she must tell him how sorry she was and fervently hope he would accept her apology.

I went too far, she silently mourned. I've killed all the feeling he ever had for me. Why am I so impulsive, so intolerant? Why, just sometimes, can't I count to ten?

But count to ten she would, Liri vowed, as reluctantly she walked down Meadowsweet Lane to keep her appointment, pausing to wonder if maybe now she could remain in Southgate Lodge.

Could she not offer the fields to Gideon and the continued use of Meadowsweet Lane? Need she sell the little house she had come to love so much? Might she not remain in Abbeyfield; stick it out in the hope that one day things might come right again?

But what was the use? Gideon had made his feelings plain. *Miss Haslington* he had mocked. *I couldn't care less what happens to Roz*, he'd said, eyes narrow with contempt.

No, she sighed as she climbed the stile, best she should make a clean break. Gideon wanted Southgate and she would tell him he could have it, lock, stock and barrel.

'You can iron out the details with the agent,' she would say. Then she would offer her hand and smile and wish him goodbye. It would quickly be over.

She looked at her watch. 7.30, exactly.

Forcing herself to be calm she crossed the paddock, climbed the dividing fence, then walked across the stableyard to the rose hedge.

7.31, and he isn't here, she fretted. So where is he, this time? Siberia? Alice Springs? She closed her eyes and willed him to come.

'Liri.'

Joyfully she spun round and looked up. He must have been standing there all the time, watching her from the open window of the hayloft bedroom.

'Come up!' he called mockingly, but she shook her head.

They would do their talking here, she insisted silently; here, at the rose hedge.

She stood very still, trying to stifle the panic inside her, listening to his descending footsteps.

'Thank you for coming,' he said softly, leaning against the iron pump, arranging his lean body comfortably. 'I appreciate it.'

'No trouble,' Liri whispered.

For just a moment they were silent, then in unison they spoke.

'I've really come here, Liri, to —'

'Gideon – it seems I made —'

'After you,' he nodded for her to continue.

'I have to say I'm sorry, Gideon.' They were being so

polite, so civilized. They were talking like strangers and acting like strangers and everything was slipping away. 'I got it wrong about you and Miss Reid. Please forgive me?'

'If you will forgive me for allowing you to get it wrong?'

'You know I will.' She gazed at her shoes. 'But about Southgate. I take it that's why we're here? Do you still want it?'

'Yes. I'll pay the asking price.'

'What if it's five thousand pounds more?'

'I want those fields.'

'Yes,' she whispered flatly, shivering in spite of herself.

'You're cold.' Instantly he removed his jacket and draped it around her shoulders.

'No!' She shrugged it away, fighting its intimacy, its masculinity. 'N-no, thanks.'

'Then come into the house. I've lit a fire in the study.'

He took her arm and she made no protest except to say, woodenly, 'I mustn't be long.'

'I won't keep you. Only as long as it takes.' His voice was deep and sensuous but she closed her mind to it. And if she tried not to look at him, tried very hard to ignore the lean, hard jawline, the eyes that could strip her soul bare; if she could shrug aside his pulsating maleness and refuse to remember how good it was to be loved by him, then she would be all right.

'You're moving in?' she asked.

'Bit by bit. I'm in no hurry. Afraid it's in a bit of a muddle.'

The room smelled of paint and new carpet and pine-logs burning. On either side of the hearth stood brass-studded leather chairs and beneath the window a desk was piled high with books.

'Make yourself comfortable.' He indicated a chair then bent to throw logs on the fire, and Liri did as he asked, nervously running her tongue around her lips.

'About buying Southgate?' She hesitated, gazing

intently at the logs as they ignited and sparked. 'You're sure?'

'I said I want it. You can tell the agent to take it off his books.'

'Good.' Still she stared into the fire. 'Well, I suppose that's it, then?' She rose to her feet and held out her hand then quickly withdrew it. She dare not touch him. 'I – I'll say goodbye.'

'Goodbye, Liri.' His voice was toneless and gave no hint of his feelings. 'I'm grateful to you.'

'Business is business,' she choked.

She had reached the hall, now. He was letting her go. He didn't care. He'd got the fields and Meadowsweet Lane and —

'Liri?'

'Yes?' Relieved, she flung round.

'Stay. For just a little while? Tell me what you plan to do.'

'Do you care, Gideon?' Her voice was tinged with bitterness.

'Of course I care. You know you can always get in touch if things shouldn't work out for you.'

'Oh, spare me the hearts and flowers!' Her voice was low with anguish. 'After all, you've got what you really wanted.'

Blindly she made for the door again but he caught and held her arm.

'I asked you to stay, Liri. Please sit down again.' He made it sound like a command, almost, and she did as he asked, balancing nervously on the edge of the chair.

'If it's about the lodge, I'm sure the agent will tell you anything else you need to know.'

'It isn't about the house. To be truthful, I don't really want it; only the land. So why don't you keep it as a gift from me – as a wedding present?'

'A w-wedding present?' Oh, but he knew how to hurt.

He didn't care at all about her engagement to James and to prove it he was handing back her house as if it were a set of pans. 'You can't mean it?'

'But I can. I do.'

'Then I'm afraid I can't accept.' Roz was speaking, now; coolly and evenly. 'I'm not getting married, you see. But put a farm-worker in it or let it off to holidaymakers. I really don't want it.'

'Not getting married?' he hissed. 'You're sure?'

'Of course I'm sure. I should know, shouldn't I?' she choked. 'James jumped the gun. He shouldn't have said what he did to the Press.'

'But does he know the engagement is off?'

'He does. We talked this afternoon,' she whispered.

'Then why on earth are you leaving, girl?'

'Why?' For the first time she allowed their eyes to meet and oh, he was still so good to look at; still had the power to arouse her. The years had made no difference to her need for him. Nothing he could do could prevent her from loving him. 'Do you think I could go on living in Abbeyfield, now?'

'What are you trying to say?' His voice was gentler, now, and he laid his hands on her shoulders. 'Tell me.'

'I'm trying to tell you —' Defiantly she shrugged away his hands. 'I'm returning to London.'

'But why? Haven't you been happy here?'

'Not really. I think I must have changed. I'm afraid Liri's gone. But you said as much, didn't you?'

'Then I was talking like a fool, because the girl in my arms acted like Liri and kissed like Liri —'

'Don't make it worse, Gideon!' Her cry was harsh with pain. 'Everything's gone wrong between us. Once we were so good together, but now all we can do is tear each other apart. I can't stay here any longer!'

'And how do you think it's been for me?' he jerked. 'Why do you think I acted as I did, last Sunday? I was wild with jealousy. I even thought you'd stage-managed the whole thing; that you'd come back just to even up the score. Then, when I started thinking straight again, I made up my mind to fight for you; convince you it was me you loved. But I read of your engagement in that blasted paper —'

'And?' Her heart was beating wildly, yet still she was afraid to hope.

'I'm trying to say that I want us to start again, Liri; to go back to the time we met at the gate of Peterkin Paddock. It was all coming good for us, that night.'

'I know,' she choked. 'It had just sunk in that you were free – after years of believing you were married.'

'Yes. I remember every word we said. I was aching to touch you. I dug my hands in my pockets, I remember. I was so scared you'd run away again.'

'I babbled on a bit, didn't I?' She laughed nervously. 'It seemed like I was dreaming and I was afraid I'd awaken. What did we talk about, Gideon?'

'Oh, about my going to Canada, and lilies and roses; about the fire at the old house. We said just about everything, except I love you.'

'I think we'd have said it, though, if Colin hadn't come.'

'Ha! His precious Flora! I left you then, didn't I, when I should have stayed?'

'Mm. I think that was when things started to go wrong. But it was my fault. I couldn't take it in,' Liri faltered. 'I was playing for time, I think, to sort myself out. And I wanted to be courted.'

'I know. But I should have told Colin to get lost. I should have made love to you there and then. Lord knows, I wanted to.'

'I wanted you to,' she whispered, her eyes on the nervously twisting fingers on her lap.

Smiling gently he gazed down at her, then taking her anxious hands in his he pulled her to her feet.

'Then why are we behaving like this? Haven't we wasted enough time already? Surely eight years is —'

'Ssssh.' Placing a finger on his lips she whispered, 'Those years are behind us. Now we can start again at the place where it ended; at the rose hedge.'

'It didn't end there, sweetheart. It took a wrong turning, perhaps, and for a time we thought we'd lost each other.'

He took her hand in his, then slid it into the pocket of his jacket and they walked slowly to the place where roses grew in tight, green buds and *liriconfancies* reflected the tints of the fading sun and threw their perfume on the evening air. Then folding her in his arms he whispered, 'I love you, Liri Haslington. I want you to marry me.'

'And I love you, Gideon, and yes, yes, yes, I *will*.'

'You're sure?' he murmured.

'Very sure. And please don't send me away! Let me stay with you tonight? I want you so much.'

'No, darling. This time around I think we should wait.'

'Wait?' Dismayed, she gazed pleadingly into his eyes. 'But it will be three weeks at the very least. Waiting that long would be torment.'

'Then shall we make it three *days?*' He was teasing her, loving her with his eyes. 'I had it in mind to get a licence from the Registrar, you see. If we applied tomorrow we could be married on Saturday.'

'So soon? You're sure?'

'I'm sure. I've already made enquiries,' he smiled. 'I haven't thought about much else since you came back to me. I want you here with me at Queen's Reach. I want to love you always; never let you out of my sight. Can't we wait three days for something as good as forever? After all the lonely years, can't we?'

'I suppose we can try,' she whispered provocatively, her lips against his ear. 'I suppose we can be delightfully old-fashioned, and wait,' she whispered demurely. 'But I won't do anything to make the waiting easy for you.' She teased his lips with her own. 'And that's a promise. I guarantee our engagement will be short but passionate.'

'Hussy,' he murmured, gathering her closer; searching hungrily for her mouth. 'Shameless, abandoned hussy.'

He kissed her then, tenderly and with wonder, but his eyes blazed dark with passion.